Being BLACK in America

MYRON VISER

Copyright © 2021 Myron Viser
All rights reserved
First Edition

PAGE PUBLISHING, INC.
Conneaut Lake, PA

First originally published by Page Publishing 2021

All rights reserved. Written permission must be secured from the publisher to use or reproduce any part of this book except for brief quotations in critical reviews or articles.

ISBN 978-1-6624-4515-6 (pbk)
ISBN 978-1-6624-4516-3 (digital)

Printed in the United States of America

Contents

Chapter 1 7
   Growing God's Economy 7
   An Abducted Nation 9
   Jacob and Esau 14
   How Esau Brings God's Hatred
   upon Himself 17
   Arsareth Becomes America 21
   Killing God's Jewels 26

Chapter 2 38
   Whitewashing Jesus Christ 38
   Margret Sanger and the Negro
   Project 41
   Unclean Foods and the Israelites 44
   Illiteracy and the Slaves 47
   Sex Farms and Buck Breaking 48
   Black Infants Used as Alligator Bait ... 50
   Show Me the Confederate Money 51
   Secret Intelligence in the US 55
   Stockholm Syndrome 58

Chapter 3 63
The 400-Year Mark, in Prophecy 63
Modern-Day Civil Rights Movement ... 64
The Rapture.. 68
The Tribulation 71
Signs of the End-Times.......................... 77
Hope for All Mankind 81
Jesus Performed Miracles.................... 84

Chapter 4 93
Crucifixion of Jesus 93
Resurrection.. 98
Jesus Returns Back to the Father....... 99
The Comforter Arrives on Earth 101
Hostility Aimed at God 104
Life in Arsareth/America—
Spiritual Egypt.. 107
Cultural Copycats 113
Celebrating God's Holidays................ 115

Chapter 5 120
Uprising of the Nation of Israelites .. 120
Forced to Change 123
Propaganda versus Police Reform ... 127
The Taking Down of Confederate
Monuments 129
Systemic Racism and Racial
Disparities... 131
Black Male Leadership........................ 134

Chapter 6 147
   Consequences for Disobedience 147
   The Captivities 149
   Abraham Fathers the Israelite
   Nation 155
   Lot Fathers the Japanese and
   Chinese Nations 157
   Esau Fathers the Edomite Nation 159
   The Ultimate Sacrifice 163
   Almighty God versus the
   Almighty Dollar 167
   The Diminishing of the Israelites
   Culture 172
   The Israelites Glorifying the World ... 178
   The Judicial System from God to
   the Israelites 181
   The Evolution of the Medical
   Logo Came from Israelites 183
   The Jewish 185
   Jewish Lives Matter 187

Chapter 7 194
   Respecting God is Expected
   from God's Chosen. 194
   The Animalistic Instinct in Us 195
   Exchanging God for Secular
   Entertainment 201

    The God of This World 205
    Black Lives Matter Movement 209
    Today's Modernized Slavery 217
    Repentance of a Nation 221
    Failed Public Relations 223

Chapter 8 228
    God's Justice for All 228
    The Great Deception 236
    Truth versus Opinions 244
    The Irony in God's Love 246

Chapter 9 255
    Today in History 255
    Readdressing Entertainment 264
    The Unity of Nations 270
    The Changing of the Guard 278

Chapter 10 284
    Social Vanity and the Pride of Life 284
    Reaping What You Sow 290
    God's Economy Trumps Man's
    Economy 297
    The Final Call for Urgency 305

Being Black In America: References 307

Chapter 1

Growing God's Economy

Growing God's economy is the primary reason for which everything is done by the Most High God Himself. The Israelites are the nation of people that God created on His land and put them in charge of all other nations to lead and fulfill his purposes. He created all nations of people for His own pleasure. Yet, the nation of Israelites is the commodity of people chosen by God to lead and grow His economy. As it is with the angels, all the nations of the world were created to serve and satisfy God's needs through obedience. That's why we exist as a civilization.

In the perfect world, God's economy thrived and grew out from Heaven to the Earth as Adam, Eve and the angels served the Lord with great passion and zeal. Their obedience to the Creator created prosperity in Heaven and on the Earth as the Lord's economy continued to grow and thrive. However, through envy of the Devil came disobedience on the part of Adam and Eve as they were tricked into breaking the law and disobeying God's command. You see, Adam and Eve were created in the image of an ever-living immortal being with immortal laws.

When the immortal laws are broken, sin, debt, and death are created, causing God's thriving economy to experience economic decline here on Earth. The act of sin committed in the Garden of Eden brought about the first debt in God's economy which caused the first economic decline in the Kingdom of God. With the presence of sin comes debt, death, and decay to all nations of people whom the Lord had originally created to live forever in perfect health and happiness. Today, all nations are deeply in debt to God due to sin. To avoid the economic collapse in the Kingdom of God, the Lord has to completely eliminate all mankind's debt of sin, through forgiveness. Nevertheless, growing God's economy flourishes through prayer and repentance of sins.

An Abducted Nation

In a perfect world, God's economy is built and operates upon fair, just, and immortal laws. However, in opposition to God's economy, the economy of this world was founded on cruel and unfair mediums of exchanges, in conjunction with the unjust laws of the land. Here in America, the unfair medium of exchanges would include the theft of land, gold, resources, in conjunction with the kidnapping, enslaving, and mistreatment of other nations of people for the purpose of numerous years of free slave labor in the building of the United States economy.

The abducted nation of Israelites would include the Negros, West Indians, Seminole Indians, Mexican Indians, North American Indians, Haitians, Puerto Ricans, Cubans, Dominicans, Argentina and Chile, Panama, and Colombia to Uruguay. The confederacy of Northern Edomites somehow believes that they are the superior nation of people on Earth, given the right to abduct other nations and force them into slavery. The abduction of God's Chosen was for the purpose of building their own wealth and power while demoralizing and degrading the Israelites. World nations are now standing at the historic crossroads of Bible prophecy.

From August 20, 1619, to August 20, 2019, marks the four-hundred-year time span of prophecy that the Nation of Israelites shall be afflicted and oppressed in a foreign land. The prophesy states that after four hundred years have passed, God will judge the nation of people that oppressed and afflicted the Children of Israel and their descendants. It would be fair to say that the judgment of God has begun in the year 2020 because the economy, which means more to the Edomites than anything else, is now suffering. In the year 2020, the United States Gross Domestic Product suffered the worst recorded drop in American history in response to the Covid-19 pandemic stay-at-home orders. The US economy has shrunk at a record-breaking 30 percent. It's not happening by coincidence; rather, it's all taking place through the Lord's prophecy. *"And he said unto Abram, Know of a surety that thy seed shall be a stranger in the land that is not theirs, and shall serve them; and they shall afflict them four hundred years. And also that nation, whom they shall serve, will I judge: and afterward they come out with great substance."* (Genesis 15: 13–14)

Some may ask the question, "Since God placed the Nation of Israelites above all other nations that He created upon the Earth, why is so much oppression being put on the Israelites, as opposed to the Edomites?" The answer is simple. God deals with nations. The Israelites were put on the Earth first, becoming the first commodities that the Lord used to grow His economy. The Israelites were the chosen nation of people held responsible for growing God's economy here on Earth.

The immortal laws and commandments of God were placed in the hands of the nation of Israelites, not in the hands of the nation of Edomites. God's laws and commandments were put in place for the purpose of growing His economy through obedience and by communication through prayer. However, being irresponsible with God's laws and commandments, the Nation of Israelites caused an economic decline in God's economy by not obeying and serving Him, creating sin-debt through self-will and disobedience. Instead of serving God the Creator, the Israelites began to serve the things that they thought they created themselves. Things that they thought would be useful in building their own economy.

Refusing to obey the Lord's commandments, the Israelites set out to build their own economy without God's laws. Nevertheless, the Nation of Israelites along with their descendants are now being held accountable to this day for their disobedience to the Lord. For this reason, four hundred years of oppression had to be carried out. The Israelites were exiled from their homeland, held captive, and taken to a foreign land to serve their enemies the Edomites, and build their economy. *"Because thou servedst not the Lord thy God with joyfulness and with gladness of heart, for the abundance of all things. Therefore shalt thou serve thine enemies which the Lord shall send against thee, in hunger, and in thirst, and in naked-*

ness, and in want of all things: and he shall put a yoke of iron upon thy neck, until he have destroyed thee" (Deuteronomy 28: 47–48).

Since the nation of Israelites chose not to serve the Lord and keep His commandments, in the year 1619, the Lord sent the Israelites' enemies against them. The Israelites were taken captive and demoralized by the Edomites who placed a yoke of iron upon their necks and shackled them in chains to be transported to America for slavery and sales. After arriving on the shores of Virginia, being held captive in a strange land, the Israelites were now in need of food, clothing, and shelter being forced to serve the nation of Edomites.

Regardless of how we are being treated here in America, being of Black Jew Israelite nationality is something to be grateful for because that was the nationality of Jesus Christ. Jesus was an Israelite, Black man, the Son of God whom sprang from the Tribe of Judah. This tribe is the most prominent among the Twelve Tribes of Israel. The name *Judah* means "lawgiver," which is relevant to who Christ is. *"For it is evident that our Lord sprang out of Judah; of which tribe Moses spoke nothing of concerning priesthood"*(Hebrews 7:14).

However, the Edomites took the Israelites from the Tribe of Judah captive. They led them away from their homeland, Egypt, and carried them over the waters by ship, arriving in chains at the shores of Jamestown, Virginia, in North America on August 20, 1619. Legally and socially acceptable here in parts of the United States of America, the families of Israelites from the Tribe of Judah were split up and used for slave labor. They were the economic engines used to build the commercial enterprise of the Edomites here in the United States.

Jacob and Esau

It's by the seed and bloodline of Abraham, Isaac, and Jacob that the Nation of Israelites was formed. Edomites—who are the descendants of Jacob's twin brother, Esau—in time, became the natural enemies of the Twelve Tribes of Israel. The bloodline of these two nations first came to pass through Isaac and Rebekah. *"And the Lord said unto her, two nations of people shall be separated from thy bowels; and the one people shall be stronger than the other people; and the elder shall serve the younger"* (Genesis 25:23). These two nations would be the Edomites and the Israelites. Long before the actual birth of Jacob, God had already chosen Jacob to be the Father of the Twelve Tribes of Israel.

"For the children being not yet born, neither having done any good or evil that the purpose of God according to election might stand, not of works, but of him that calleth" (Romans 9:11). The younger brother Jacob had been destined to become the Father of the Israelites. The birth of Esau, father of the Edomites, marked the beginning of the nation of Edomites. *"And when her days to be delivered were fulfilled, behold there were twins in her womb. And the first came out red all over like a hairy garment; and they called his name Esau. And after that came his brother out, and his hands took hold on Esau's heel; and his name was called Jacob"* (Genesis 25: 24–26).

These two children, Jacob and Esau, represent the beginning of what God calls two separate nations of people on Earth, and He chose one over the other. The Bible states that Esau, the first of Rebekah's twins came out red all over. Esau, like many so-called Caucasian babies, is born with an overall red complexion. On the account of their own complexions, the nation of Edomites named themselves Caucasian, and prefer to be called White. On the account of the skin color of the Israelites, the Edomites invented bywords such as Negros, Niggers, Mexicans, and Indians to identify and denigrate God's Chosen people, the Israelites.

By the way, the Lord never created *Black humans*, neither did he create *White humans*. Meant to identify and divide nations, the bywords *Black* and *White* were invented by the Edomites as their classifications of people. Even though the first man Adam was created by God from dirt, which is mostly the color brown, the invented byword or classification Black (Negro) is seen as being dirty or filthy human beings. While Whites (Caucasian) were seen as being the clean and the pure nation of human beings. Whites being prideful, feel superior to all the other nations that God created. God's Chosen people are seen and treated by the Edomites in America as the inferior race of people created by God here on Earth, which is the opposite of God's word.

How Esau Brings God's Hatred upon Himself

He was a prideful cunning hunter, a thief as well as a murderer. *"And the boys grew; and Esau was a cunning hunter, a man of the field; and Jacob was a plain man, dwelling in the tents"* (Genesis 25:27). Being prideful, Esau did not want his Father's inheritance. That's why he so easily sold his birthright to his brother Jacob. Prior to Esau selling his birthright, Esau had returned from hunting and killing King Nimrod in the fields. He was very tired and hungry from mortally fighting the two bodyguards, and escaping from Nimrod's men. He reached his father's house and stood in front of Jacob exhausted and asked him to feed him the red pottage that Jacob had prepared. That's when Jacob responded by saying, "Sell me your birthright and I will feed you."

Thinking his life was in danger, on impulse, despising his birthright anyway, Esau swore to Jacob that he was exchanging his birthright for the red pottage. At this point, Esau knew that he lost his birthright and the blessings of his Father. Esau, knowing that he had just killed King Nimrod, was frightened that he was about to be killed. Authorized by a Holy God, the birthright honors the rights and privileges of the first-born son after the death of a Father to a double portion of the Father's inheritance. Esau's ungratefulness and disrespect for human life was displeasing in the sight of God.

Second Samuel in the Old Testament gives reference to the Book of Jasher, which gives the account of the murders. *"Also he bade them to teach the children of Judah the use of the bow: behold it is written in the Book of Jasher"* (Second Samuel 1:18). To further enrage a Holy God, Esau stole the holy garments that were passed on to King Nimrod from Adam. *"And Nimrod and two of his men that were with him came to the place where they were, when Esau started suddenly from his lurking place and drew his sword and hastened and ran to Nimrod and cut off his head. And Esau fought a desperate fight with the two men that were with Nimrod and when they called out to him, Esau turned to them and smote them to death with his sword"* (Jasher 27:7–8).

Murdering King Nimrod and cutting off his head in the hunting fields was not satisfying enough for Esau. To further satisfy himself, Esau stripped and stole the garments off King Nimrod's lifeless body. These were the Holy garments of skin that the Lord had made for Adam and Eve when they left The Garden of Eden. The Seventh Chapter of Jasher, (the book mentioned in Second Samuel 1:18) gives the accounts of the Holy garments of skin that God Himself made for Adam and Eve after leaving The Garden of Eden.

> *And the garments of skin which God made for Adam and his woman, when they went out of the Garden were given to Cush. And after the death*

of Adam and his woman the garments were given to Enoch, the son of Jared. And when Enoch was taken up to God, he gave them to Methuselah his son. And at the death of Methuselah, Noah took them and brought them to the Ark, and they went with him until he went out of the Ark. And in their going out, Ham stole the garments from Noah his father, and he took them and hid them from his brothers. And Ham begot his first-born Cush, he gave him the garments in secret, and they were Cush many days. And Cush also concealed them from his sons and brothers. And when Cush had begotten Nimrod he gave him those garments through his love for him. And Nimrod grew up. And when he was twenty years old he put on those garments. And Nimrod became strong when he put on the gar-

ments. Nimrod ruled with the garments which God made for Adam and his woman. (Jasher 7: 24–30)

And Esau took these garments and ran into the city on the account of Nimrods men, and he came into his father's house wearied and exhausted from the fight and he was ready to die through grief when he approached his brother Jacob and sat before him. (Jasher 27:11)

Arsareth Becomes America

Passed down from Esau, the father of the Nation of Edomites, the dispositional genetic hereditary traits of their ancestors are formed. Their traits are in the genes and there is not much they can do to change those traits. Naturally feeling entitled to hunt, steal and kill, the mentality of the Edomites continued to surface through violence against the ten tribes of Israel in Arsareth whose lives did not matter to them. Any nation founded in the blood of the Israelites could never be righteous in God's sight. The White man, which the Lord calls Edomites, have stolen property from the Israelites by seizing 3.8 million square miles of their native land Arsareth, which had already been occupied by ten tribes of Israel when the Edomites claimed to have discovered it.

The United States of America, previously known as Arsareth is all stolen land. The method used for seizing the land occupied by the Israelites was murdering thousands of innocent Israelite men, women, and children of the ten tribes of Israel. Upon the arrival of Christopher Columbus in 1492, his men changed the name of the stolen land from Arsareth, to America. This stolen land marked the beginning and is the root cause of racial disparities of the Israelites in America today. Later the Edomites passed laws to remove the Israelites from their native homeland Arsareth by enslaving the people, they sold them like animals, separating the children from their families, in conjunction with taking away their languages and cultures. Once they enslaved the Natives of Arsareth they enslaved other Israelites from abroad.

The economy of the new Arsareth/America was built on the backs and the bloodshed of the Nation of Israelites. Being that it's God's decision that one nation of people would serve the other nation of people as economic slaves, the Israelites are the industrial slaves for the corporation of the Edomites. It's the duty of Israelites to know and trust that God will triumph over their enemies and will take action in His time.

Because we failed to joyfully serve God and keep His commandments in the beginning, as unfair as it may sound, servitude to the Edomites is the one primary lesson that God is teaching the Nation of Israelites. However, it is promised, one moment in the Kingdom of God will pay for all the suffering and affliction experienced here on Earth. Servitude to God by the nation of Israelites is that which quickly moves the Lord to take action on our behalf. Here in Arsareth/America, and in many other parts of the world, the laws of the land in which we live were put into place by the posterity of Esau.

The fruit does not fall too far from the tree. Personality traits have a genetic basis. The Edomites are a nation of people that feel legally entitled to do as they please. Their temperament makes it difficult for them to get along with the other nations of people in the world. Especially, God's chosen people, the Israelites. Israelites are living in a foreign land where they are legally being shot dead in the streets by the people that they pay their taxes to. The people whose job is to protect them. The judicial system in the United States was set up to cater to the needs of the nation of Edomites.

The corrupt judicial system in the United States is designed to work even more violently against the Israelites. We are unfairly being treated as partial United States citizens politically, socially, and economically. Israelites can't seek legal financial and medical help without having the Edomites working against them in one way or the other.

We are still being treated as second-class citizens by the laws.

As far as citizenship, think about it. It's very unlikely that the people whose ancestors were taken captive into this foreign land to be enslaved, raped, beaten, and lynched could become true citizens, and as such be entitled to all the full rights and privileges of the nation of Edomites. If the Israelites were really citizens of the United States, by law, the Edomites are entitled to protect us. Being that the citizenship of the Israelites is in Heaven, they have rights according to God's laws, and their claims are recognizable and enforced by His law. As Israelites, it is our function to support and defend the Laws of God. *"For our citizenship is in Heaven; from whence also we look for the Saviour, the Lord Jesus Christ"* (Philippians 3:20).

I remember my humble beginnings in the early sixties being in first grade. Our teachers would have their Holy Bible on their desks and we would pray before the beginning of class. Prayer in school being instrumental to God's economy was short-lived because prayer was eliminated from public schools in 1962, thanks to the White atheist Madeline Murray O'Hare. Taking the place of prayer, we started reciting the United States Pledge of Allegiance. The teachers drilled that pledge of Allegiance into our heads daily. Being a young innocent happy child, I really believed in the last sentence that stated, "and liberty and justice for all."

Growing up in the early seventies, as I got older, I began to notice that when I turned on the TV, I never saw ourselves as a Negro race featured on the television programs, except for Saturdays, on the *Soul Train* dance show and in situation comedies. My race of people not being widely represented and spoken for was beginning to raise a red flag in my young mind. At the time, I knew something was wrong, but I was too young to figure out that it was racial discrimination.

Killing God's Jewels

One tragic event that I can remember, as if it just happened yesterday, was on April 4, 1968. Reverend Doctor Martin Luther King Jr. was assassinated by the racist James Earl Ray. Reverend Doctor

Martin Luther King Jr. was standing on the balcony outside his room at the Lorraine Motel in Memphis Tennessee just after 6:00 p.m. He was fatally shot to death with a single bullet. As a Negro teenager, witnessing this event made things appear as though Negros were the most insignificant race of people in the United States.

Do you remember these words during a presidential campaign? *"Yes, We Can Change"* Even living in the time when Barack Obama, a Black man, was President of the United States, social and institutional systems still privileged Whites over people of color. White Supremacy here in America still persists and has even worsened. Income gaps, racial disparities, and police brutality are still the American way. The principle of life, liberty, and the pursuit of happiness... Really?

The militarization of the police departments has led to excessive use of force against people of color. One instance taking place on May 25, 2020. The inhumane act occurred as the White police officer, Derek Chauvin, unrelentingly pressed his knee against George Floyd's neck. All of this while Floyd was handcuffed and face down on the pavement which prevented him from breathing, and therefore triggering asphyxiation. Thus, executing George Floyd within eight minutes and forty-five seconds while he pleaded for breath. Three other Esau cops stood by watching. The police officer's sense of superiority ended another Israelite's life. It was like a scene in the animal kingdom watching a python seizing and constricting its prey.

    As much anger as this act provoked, vengeance is the Lord's. We as a people are to love our enemies. Loving your enemies are easy words to say, yet difficult to practice. George Floyd, like any other human being does not have the luxury or right to hate anyone. Only God the Creator has that luxury and right. *"I have loved you said the Lord. Yet ye say. Wherein has thou loved us? Was not Esau Jacob's brother? Saith the Lord: Yet I loved Jacob. And I hated Esau, and laid his mountains and his heritage waste in the dragons of the wilderness"* (Malachi 1:2–3). The Israelite Jesus Christ, Son of God, from the tribe of Judah said, *"But I say unto you, Love your enemies, bless them that curse you, do good to them that hate you, and pray for them which despitefully use you, and persecute you"* (Matthew 5:44). Loving our enemies is extremely difficult to do, but according to the Holy Bible, it is the only way to salvation.

However, in some instances, loving your enemies (the people paid to protect and serve) can give you a false sense of trust in them, eventually, leading to deadly consequences. When will there be justice for people of color? The list goes on and on. It was the seventeenth day of July in 2014, another unarmed Black citizen of the United States, Eric Garner, was selling single cigarettes on the sidewalk when police officer, Daniel Pantaleo, tackled him to the ground. The officer put Mr. Garner in an illegal chokehold preventing him from breathing, therefore, triggering suffocation. Several other officers were restraining him as Daniel choked him to death. The White police officer Daniel Pantaleo was acquitted of wrongful death.

It's not always the fault of state law enforcement officers. White supremacists feel entitled to savagely take the lives of people of color as well. Another grim reminder is the inhumane murder of another Black Israelite, James Byrd Jr. He was savagely murdered by three White supremacists on the seventh day of June in 1998. The three White supremacists John King, Shawn Berry, and Lawrence Brewer chained James Byrd Jr. to the back of a pickup truck. They proceeded to drag him to death as they drove for three miles down Huff Creek Road, an asphalt road in Jasper Texas. The head and the right arm of James Byrd Jr. were severed off his body during the three-mile dragging.

You may ask yourself, "Where is all this hatred coming from?" I can tell you that it goes a lot deeper than skin color. I hope that you are sitting down as you read the next two paragraphs. You are hated because the Edomites know who you are. (Negros, West Indians, Haitians, Puerto Ricans, Cubans, Dominicans, Seminole Indians, North American Indians, Argentina and Chile, Guatemala to Panama, Colombia to Uruguay, and Mexican Indians.) You are hated by all other nations of the world because you are the Israelites.

Jesus Christ, the Israelite from the Tribe of Judah said in John 15:18–19, *"If the world hate you, you know that it hated me before it hated you. If you were of the world, the world would love its own; but because you are not of the world, but I have chosen you out of the world, therefore the world hateth you."* The nation of Israelites is God's chosen people. You see, the people who are being persecuted by the White men, the Israelites, don't know who they are. The Edomites on the other hand know exactly who we are. That's why Israelites are being persecuted. *"For thou art an holy people unto the Lord thy God, and the Lord hath chosen thee to be a peculiar people unto himself, above all the nations that are upon the earth"* (Deuteronomy 14:2).

The Israelites beginning with the Tribe of Judah, are God's precious jewels. The Tribe of Judah is the Negro tribe that Jesus Christ the Son of God sprang forth from. Taking the lives of God's precious jewels is the priority of the cunning hunters of the generations of Esau, the Father of the Edomites. They acquit themselves for the unlawful killings of other human beings by structuring the laws of the Department of Justice in ways to protect Caucasians from their own laws. Black police officers in America are not acquitted of murdering Caucasians.

Call for justice. We need justice for the senseless shooting of unarmed Trayvon Martin. A seventeen-year-old teenager just walking the streets of Florida, minding his own business, was shot to death by George Zimmerman on February 26, 2012. The neighborhood watch person George Zimmerman got away with the homicide of an innocent young Black man. Zimmerman was *acquitted due to insufficient evidence.*

Call for justice. We need justice for the senseless shooting of unarmed John Crawford III who was killed by a White Esau police officer at Walmart in Dayton Ohio, on April 5, 2014. There was no confrontation between John Crawford and the officer. John Crawford was in the store holding a toy BB gun as he was gunned down by the people that he trusted would protect him. *The White police officer was not charged with homicide.*

Call for justice. We need justice for the senseless shooting of unarmed Michael Brown on April 9, 2015. The unarmed Black man was shot to death by Ferguson police officer Darren Wilson. *The White police officer was not charged for the murder.*

Call for justice. We need justice for the senseless shooting of unarmed Black man Donte Hamilton, on April 30, 2014. He was fatally shot fourteen times by a police officer Christopher Manney in a Milwaukee park. It was determined that Donte Hamilton wasn't doing anything wrong. *The White police officer was not charged.*

Call for justice. We need justice for the senseless shooting of unarmed Ezell Ford, shot on August 11, 2014, in Florence California. The twenty-five-year-old mentally ill Black man was shot and killed by a White police officer in front of his family. *The White police officer was not charged.*

Call for justice. We need justice for the senseless shooting of unarmed Dante Parker, killed with a Taser gun by police. The incident happened on August 12, 2014, in the state of California. The Black man died in police custody after being repeatedly stunned by a Taser gun. *The White police officer was not charged.*

Call for justice. We need justice for the senseless police brutality that killed the unarmed Black female, Tanisha Anderson. On November 13, 2014, Tanisha Anderson died after White officers in Cleveland slammed her head on the pavement while taking her into custody. *The White police officers were not charged.*

Call for justice. We need justice for the senseless shooting of unarmed Tamir Rice in November of 2014. The twelve-year-old boy was killed by White Cleveland police officers after the officers mistook his toy gun for a real weapon. *The two White police officers Timothy Loehmann and Frank Garmback were not charged.*

Call for justice. We need justice for the senseless shooting of unarmed Black man Rumain Brisbon. He was shot and killed on December 2, 2014, by the police officer who mistook a pill bottle for a weapon. *The White police officer Mark Rino was not charged.*

Call for justice. We need justice for the senseless homicide of unarmed Black man Phillip White. Happening on March 31, 2015, in Vineland New Jersey, Phillip White died in police custody. The video footage showed a police dog biting Phillip White while he was on the ground. *The White police officers were not charged.*

Call for justice. We need justice for the senseless shooting of unarmed Black man Walter Scott. This happened on April 4, 2015, in Charleston, South Carolina. Walter Scott was pulled over for a brake light that was not working. Police Officer Michael Sloger fatally shot Walter Scott three times in the back, one time in the head, and once in the buttocks killing him. Michael Sloger handcuffed Walter Scott's hands behind his back after shooting him as he laid on the ground dying. *The White police officer was sentenced to twenty years and released in two years.* Early release of police officer Michael Sloger gives him another eighteen years to commit more crimes against people of color.

Call for justice. We need justice for the senseless killing of unarmed Black female Breonna Taylor, on March 30, 2019. She was shot eight times and killed by three White policemen unlawfully raiding her apartment while she was asleep. Unarmed Breonna Taylor an EMT, was startled out of her sleep by three plain-clothed White police officers kicking in her door. Not announcing that they were policemen, they opened fire executing an innocent Black woman. More than twenty-five bullets hit objects in her home. *Myles Cosgrove, Jonathan Mattingly, and Brett Hankison were not charged for the brutal murder.*

Unfortunately, it took the Louisville Police Chief over a year to fire any of the officers involved. On September 16, 2020, a twelve-million-dollar settlement was reached to pay to Breonna Taylor's family. Yet, after the payoff of twelve million dollars, the policemen involved with Breonna's murder are still not charged for her senseless death. To pay off a family that type of money seems to me to be admitting to the wrongful murder of Ms. Taylor, however, the city claimed no wrongdoing.

As a mockery for the justice of Breonna, former Detective Brett Hankinson was indicted on three felony charges. Not for killing Breonna, but because three of the thirty-two bullets that were fired entered into an apartment occupied by a White man, White woman, and White child, endangering them. In the end, no justice was served because Brett Hankinson, Myles Cosgrove, and Jonathan Mattingly, were charged for Breonna's wrongful death.

Nothing is actually being done in America to obtain justice for Blacks being killed by White police officers. It's been happening for decades now. Political activism seems to be a waste of time. All the protesting in the world doesn't seem to make a difference. We are being told again and again to get over it! We can do absolutely nothing to stop the senseless killings of these unarmed Black citizens but wait on the Lord. The Bible says in Romans 12:19, *"Dearly beloved, avenge not yourselves, but rather give place unto wrath; for it is written, Vengeance is mine; I will repay, saith the Lord."* Until the Lord returns, we must prepare our minds for hundreds or more cases of vicious and wanton police murders.

Chapter 2

Whitewashing Jesus Christ

Being Black in America is based on the truth. Trillions of American dollars have been spent in the Arsareth/American economy for the purpose of hiding the truth from the Nation of Israelites. It's better for Israelites to educate their children at home. Hiding the truth involved spending trillions of US dollars for the whitewashing of Jesus Christ, the Son of God. To portray Jesus Christ, the Son of God, to be a blonde-haired, blue-eyed Caucasian White man is heresy. Oh! It doesn't matter if Jesus Christ, the Son of God, was Black or White? The truth always matters!

    Otherwise, they would have portrayed him as a dark-skinned man with wooly hair as it is written in the Old and New Testaments. Catering to the wants and needs of the

Caucasian nation of White people, whitewashing, increases the relevance and prominence of that nation of people above the Israelites. In fact, whitewashing, in the portrayal of Jesus Christ and many other Israelites as White people, alters the original truth written in the pages of the Holy Bible. It misrepresents the Negro, Hispanic, and Native Americans who are the Israelites.

The whitewashing of Jesus Christ, the Son of God, is blasphemy of the Holy Spirit. It is also an abomination to portray Jesus Christ to be an Edomite. A descendant of Esau. Blasphemy of the Holy Spirit is the only sin we can't repent from. On Judgment Day, we will be held accountable. Jesus Christ was a dark-skinned Israelite from the Tribe of Judah. In the New Testament, the scripture reads, *"His head and his hairs were white like wool, as white as snow; and his eyes were as a flame of fire; And his feet were like fine brass, as if they burned in a furnace; and his voice as the sound of many waters"* (Revelation 1: 14–15). Again, in the Old Testament, worded slightly different in reference to the texture of his hair, the scripture reads, *"I beheld till the thrones were cast down, and the Ancient of days did sit, whose garment was white as snow, and the hair on his head like the pure wool: his throne was like a fiery flame, and his wheels as burning fire"* (Daniel 7:9).

Okay, let's get right back to the truth about skin color. We should start from the very beginning. Jesus Christ was born as an infant in Bethlehem. They called him Emmanuel. King Herod knew that Jesus, the newborn King, was about to be born. That's when, out of jealousy and hatred, he commanded that all male infants that were born in that region be killed at once. The caring father and mother knew that they had to protect their son. So they took baby Jesus to Egypt, a civilization of dark-skinned people and hid Him in plain sight. By being among many other dark-skinned people in Egypt, the infant would fit right in, and safely be concealed. By bloodline, Jesus is a Jew from the Tribe of Judah.

I can remember growing up as a child opening up our eight-and-a-half-by-eleven-inch family Bible. On the second page of the Bible was the eight-and-a-half-by-eleven-inch, picture of White Jesus. After researching the photo as an adult, I found that it was the photo of Cesare Borgia. He was an Italian White man. The son of Polk Alexander VI who died on March 11, 1507. Not knowing any better, just as all children and most adults, the photo of a White man in the front of the Holy Bible would give them the false impression that Jesus was a White man. Jesus's followers, the twelve Israelite Jew Disciples, are also being whitewashed throughout history by the Edomites.

Margret Sanger and the Negro Project

The family linage and ethnicity of Jesus Christ, in relation to the nation of Blacks, and all others from the Twelve Tribes of Israel, is the key to understanding the world conspiracy. The true Jews, Israelites, have been targeted for extermination by the Edomites for years. They have the upper hand, as well as being in charge of the laws of the land. Let me ask the question. "Do you know anyone that has received the assistance from the organization called Planned Parenthood?"

Here's a little background on the organization. In the year 1939, the founder of

Planned Parenthood, White supremacist Margret Sanger, founded the American Birth Control League. She strongly believed that her race was superior! The agenda of Margret Sanger was solely to exterminate the Negro population. According to the Legislative Affiliate of Family Research Council, Margret Sanger said, "Blacks are human weeds that need to be exterminated and we do not want the word to go out that we want to exterminate the Negro population."

Since the year 1973, around nineteen million Black babies have been aborted, mostly by the Planned Parenthood Organization "Negro Project" which is funded by the US Federal Government. In the year 1926, Margret Sanger was the featured speaker at the women's auxiliary meeting of the Ku Klux Klan in Silver Lake, New Jersey. Legal extermination of the Black race is one of many reasons Israelites are still a minority in this country.

In addition, our voices are being silenced by the disproportional number of Israelites imprisoned in America. Blacks and Hispanics males make up 28 percent of the population. Yet, we make up 58 percent of the people who are incarcerated. Not because Israelites commit more crimes, but because the judicial system is racially and financially stacked against us. Edomites account for 64 percent of the US population, but only 30 percent of people in jails or prisons.

Again, without a doubt, the judicial system in this country is racially and financially biased. The rich and the Edomites get acquitted, while the poor and Israelites get convicted.

Police and prosecutors are operating above the law. They will do as they please. Pig Laws, used to imprison Blacks, are backed by the US justice system. The laws (Pig Laws) unfairly penalize the poor and Black Israelite Jews by legally treating misdemeanors or trivial offences as felonies. On top of that, Blacks and Hispanics are disproportionately being imprisoned because police and prosecutors are not being held accountable for their actions. This leads to injustices and ends in grievances.

Grievances are then extended to the families of the incarcerated. Sometimes children have to watch their parents as they are being taken away by the authorities. Thus, suffering from years of physical and emotional trauma. Financial instability is one of the first things that plague the families of those that are imprisoned. For prisoners that happen to be parents, being separated from their children is like serving a double sentence. Abandoned children without parents as role models tend to negatively act out. For parents, the trauma associated with not being able to watch their children grow up into adulthood is endless. Meanwhile, being concerned with how their children are being raised without them takes a toll on the incarcerated as well as their families.

Unclean Foods and the Israelites

Another primary reason the Israelites are a minority in the United States is that during the Atlantic Slave Trade, the Edomites forced slaves to eat their unclean foods and scraps for centuries. This diet has been passed down from one generation to the next. Hogs, especially, were plentiful on the plantations and the slave-masters made sure that nothing was wasted. The parts of the pig that the slave masters and their families despised, is what slaves were forced to eat.

According to the Bible, swine is an unclean food for God's chosen people, the Israelites. High in fat and cholesterol, the toxins along with the bacteria associated with swine spreads numerous fatal diseases, including hepatitis and high blood pressure, the silent killer. Israelite slaves were forced to eat hog ears, pig's feet, along with the intestines. This led to the unhealthy posterity of the Israelite nation. The Lord said in Deuteronomy chapter 14: 2–3, *"For thou art an Holy People unto the Lord thy God, and the Lord hath chosen thee to be a peculiar people unto himself, above all nations that are upon the earth. Thou shalt not eat any abominable thing."*

Fatty pork was the staple food and the main meat available to the Israelite slaves. It is my belief that the Edomites knew and understood the devastation they were imparting to the slaves as they had read the same scripture I just quoted. Over the years, the abominable diet introduced to slaves has been passed down through generations. Swine is still being consumed by American Israelites due to Biblical ignorance.

Eating seafood that lacks fins and scales is another abomination often committed by the Israelites. Shrimp, lobster, and crabs do not have fins and scales. They are the roaches of the sea. These three scavengers crawl around on the bottom of the sea floor, eating dead animals, trash, and anything their claws can grab. Shellfish, such as oysters, clams, and mussels, filters the bacteria out of the waters. They are also created for the purpose of cleaning the sea floor. These foods are considered delicacies by the Edomites. The Bible makes it clear that other nations can indulge in unclean foods, but the Israelites, God's chosen people, cannot. Chapter 14 in the book of Deuteronomy devotes scriptures to the education of what is considered clean and unclean.

Illiteracy and the Slaves

The inability to read this book and other such publications has crippled generations of Israelites. Illiteracy is the venom the Edomites used to poison the progression of the minds of the Israelites. Knowledge is power, and the absence of knowledge is ignorance. The truth is, economics and education go hand-in-hand. Getting ahead in America has always required literacy. In the year 1740, the first law was passed in South Carolina prohibiting the education of slaves. In the early 1800s, here in the United States, Missouri, and other states prohibited assembling for teaching slaves to read or write. The offense was punishable by a fine and imprisonment. It wasn't until 1855 that the Massachusetts Legislature allowed Blacks to be educated in public schools.

Racism is a social pandemic that has plagued the United States for hundreds of years. Anything that could eradicate slavery was made illegal in the South. Being able to read and write was deemed as a threat to the institution of slavery. Israelites being able to read and write in the United States was a threat because literacy would make them aware of their rights. Literacy would have given them the power to contact the appropriate institutions that could defend their rights. Many enslaved people taught themselves and each other how to read and write in secret. They feared severe punishment from their slave master if caught.

Sex Farms and Buck Breaking

Another way the Israelites were demoralized and controlled by the Edomites was by buck breaking. During slavery, the homosexual slave owners purchased well-endowed male slaves to engage in sexual acts. The practice became so common that they started sex farms on plantations. They would break the spirit and courage of slaves by viciously beating and raping them in private and publicly. They humiliated, whipped, and sodomized the strongest males in front of their own families and other slaves to instill fear and flaunt their dominance.

According to the Atlanta Black Star, at the age of thirteen, slave owners would impregnate enslaved women. The women were expected to have four to five children by the age of twenty. These children, fathered by the slave owners and fellow slaves would be raised up to become slaves. Male slaves at the age of fourteen would be assessed for breeding, judged by the size of their genitals.

The ones that did not meet the standard would be castrated and often resold for farm labor. Male slaves deemed worthy to reproduce were expected to impregnate twelve females per year for five years.

The deemed-to-be-pretty female slaves were made house niggers. However, they often suffered at the hands of the master's wife including the beheading of their child conceived by rape by the slave master. Sex farms were established on plantations. Male and female slaves were forced to have sexual relations with each other whether they were family or not. The slave master and his friends would watch for their own sadistic pleasure and often participate in sexual acts. What a cultural shock to the Israelites.

Black Infants Used as Alligator Bait

Speaking of atrocious and heinous acts, according to the *Miami New Times* in the early 1900s, Israelite babies were used as alligator bait. The cunning hunters of the descendants of Esau would place Black infants at the water banks. They placed ropes around the neck and waist of innocent Black children and the Edomites watched them cry and splash about until an alligator honed in on them. Once the baby was in the mouth of the alligator, the Edomite hunters would kill the alligator, sacrificing the life of the Israelite babies to make alligator shoes and purses.

These are just a few of the atrocities and evil acts committed against the Israelites. Yet there are so many more. Some have been documented, some have not. The reality is that Israelites have been treated barbarously for far too long. Just as we are saved by the stripes of Jesus Christ, the Edomites will be condemned by their treatment of God's chosen people. Whites may not realize it, but they are diminishing their economy with every brutal action against God's precious jewels.

Show Me the Confederate Money

Looking at money from the historical point of view is vital in understanding why it looks the way it does. Money is the primary resource used in the building of the US economy. The history in its design is vital to the understanding of why its design hasn't changed over the centuries. The featured photos of White people on paper currency and coins in the United States of America are purposely there to flaunt racism, power, and White supremacy. The theme of money design is slavery. Like Confederate monuments, Edomites honored slave masters to guarantee their exploits would not be forgotten.

Centered on the one-dollar bill is the photo of the first president of the United States, George Washington. Our founding US president was the owner of slaves before, during, and after his Presidency. George Washington, along with many other Presidents of the US, were slave masters.

President Washington had over one hundred enslaved human beings. His wife set them free one year after his death. For centuries now, all citizens making money transactions in the United States economy has used paper currency. For hundreds of years, paper currency had to be used daily to purchase items for all the necessities of life.

The slave owner President Andrew Jackson's photo is featured on the $20 bill. Being president from 1829 until 1837, he owned a cotton plantation. He enslaved over a hundred Black men, women, and children to work his fields. The source of his income was literally built on the backs and bloodshed of the Israelites. With his callous attitudes toward slavery, he chose not to free his slaves, even in his will, as it was customary to do.

Speaking of whitewashing American history, the only person of color to be depicted on currency is Abraham Lincoln. Unbeknownst to most people, Lincoln was the first Black President of the United States. Like many Israelite's accomplishments, his race has been whitewashed by history. Most people in the world are unaware that his father was a Black man. Though they honored him by placing his likeness on a coin, for the sake of White supremacy, because Abraham Lincoln was a Black man, they put him on the lowest denomination they could spend, the copper one-cent piece.

Over the centuries, these White faces of slave owners on the money that we use daily were constant reminders of racism, power, and White supremacy. In reference to the previous statement concerning Black faces not being featured on money, true understanding of the viewpoint comes through being Black in America. We all earn and we all have to spend money to survive. Therefore, honorees on money should be as diverse as the people who spend it. Why haven't the face of Barack Obama, the second Black President of the United States been featured on paper currency? One of the reasons is that a petition was never implemented in his favor.

What good would it have done anyway, because a petition was implemented in the favor of Harriet Tubman to feature her face on the $20 bill. It's the pride in the hearts of the Edomites in control of manufacturing the currency in this country that rejects Black faces being featured on the money we spend. I believe that the Edomites would have been willing to feature Harriet Tubman's face on the penny, as they featured the Black President Abraham Lincoln. Our current generations have become desensitized to the stigma of slavery. Young Israelites don't recognize the historical threat associated with "White faces" being honored on money. To our youth, money is simply currency, but it runs much deeper than that.

Here in America, just as the whitewashing of Jesus Christ makes the Caucasians feel superior to other nations of people, the Edomites also feel superior with their faces on currency. The Caucasian faces featured on money is there to intimidate other nations of people into believing that they are inferior to Caucasians. Whitewashing currency also increases the relevance and prominence of the Edomite nation of people over the Israelites as well as other nations of people. Being a Black person in America we have to work our fingers to the bone to earn our money that features only White faces. Then we have to turn around and pay it back to the Edomites just to survive.

All of the currency earned by the people of color has White faces plastered on every single bill, from the one-dollar bill all the way up to the hundred. Israelites and people of color spend just as much money as anyone else and would like to see prominent people that look like them featured on some of it, other than the worthless penny. When the Edomites love money so much that they refuse to feature the faces of Israelites on it, the issue needs to be addressed. *"If you can't relate, you can't debate."*

Secret Intelligence in the US

The secret elite societies in the United States are the main funders that promote inequality among the people. In fact, certain sectors of the US government are not working in favor of the general population of the people. Instead, the government is working for the wealthy. Stemming out of hate, and happening for centuries now, these secret elite societies has characterized the Negro

Israelites as human trash. Behind closed doors, in secrecy, financial and judicial systems are working against the best interest of the poor and the Israelites.

These secret unknown societies in the United States have played their role in funding and in the conspiracy to discriminate against the Israelites. Through secret proceedings and oaths, it's agreed that in order to keep receiving the funds flowing from the secret societies, the judicial system is not to be scrutinized for the injustices against the poor and Israelites. It's through secret proceedings and secret oaths, that the judicial system is able to flaunt injustices against the poor and people of color. For hundreds of years now, secrecy and loyalty has made infiltration impossible.

Economic disparities in the United States between the Israelites and the Edomites has resulted from long periods of systemic racism. Over an extended period of time the Edomites have accumulated more wealth than Israelites. Slavery legally prevented the Israelites from building wealth. White people make more money while the

Israelites have to work twice as hard, at the same job, for less pay.

The hierarchy is as follows: White men make the most money, followed by White women. Black females earn more than Black males. Black males, an endangered species, are the lowest on the totem pole. Within the past fifty-two years, not much has changed. The worsening racial wealth gap remains as wide as it was in 1968, and is still deepening. Data from the US Census Bureau reveals that Black wealth is about 9 percent of that of Whites. Who do you think owns all of the tall buildings and skyscrapers in the US?

The reasons I said Black males are an endangered species run deep. I've mentioned many ways. In addition to hundreds of thousands being killed in the slave trade, hundreds of thousands more of Black men were put on the frontline, and killed in the United States military. Add Black-on-Black crime, we are helping to exterminate ourselves. We are being hunted down and killed in the streets by rogue cops for no reason. Pair all of this with poor diets and limited access to health care, it is frankly a wonder we have not been completely eliminated from the United States.

According to NAACP.org, African Americans are incarcerated at five times the rate as of Whites. Israelite males represent the highest category of people incarcerated in the US. The imprisonment rate of African American women is twice that of White women. African American children represent 32 percent of children who are arrested and 42 percent of those who are detained, and 52 percent of those whose case are judicially waived to criminal court.

Stockholm Syndrome

Unfortunately, too many Israelites suffer from Stockholm syndrome. This is defined as the feeling of trust or affection felt by victims toward their captor. Also, an emotional bond or psychological alliance with their captors during captivity. Israelites trusting in the United States Constitution is a symptom of the Stockholm syndrome. The US Constitution was never meant to include us. Written in the year 1787, while the Blacks were in slavery, the United

States Constitution served as the supreme law in the US for "We, the people," the nation of Edomites—White people only. The Constitution does not include serving the Israelites.

It was never a part of their plan to let enslaved captives become citizens and have access to the same privileges as the so-called true citizens of the United States. *"Envy not the oppressor and choose none of his ways"* (Proverbs 3:31). Israelites don't want to take anything away from Edomites, we just want the same freedom, respect, and privileges as other citizens of the US. As I was growing up in the sixties, during the time of segregation, my father used to tell us that the Three-Fifths Clause of the United States Constitution was being used by White people on his job to taunt Black people. White men on the job would sometimes say to my father and other Black coworkers that they were only three fifths of a man.

In the early fifties, my mother and father had to drink from the colored water fountains and use the colored bathrooms. My parents mentioned that when traveling with their parents and us, in the late 1940s through the late 1960s, because we were Black, they had to use the Negro Motorist Green Book. It mapped out places safe for Israelites to find food, gas, and lodging. Also to keep Negros from being harassed, without cause, by the White citizens and Edomite law enforcement officers.

The same harassment exists on a different level in the White House. Other examples of systemic racism are seen coming from Republican parties in the White House. The Constitution states that one must be a US Citizen in order to serve as the President. The second Black president of the United States Barack Obama was falsely accused by President Donald Trump of not being a United States citizen in order to have him removed from office. A few years later, while sitting president, Donald Trump accused Kamala Harris, the first Black female vice president nominee of the United States of the same thing. Another failed attempt of keeping the Blacks at bay through systemic racism.

Jesus advises us to love our enemies and that vengeance is His. Yet, on the other hand He teaches us to stand up for what is righteous. It's hard to love your enemy when you are slammed face down on hot pavement, with an officer kneeling on your neck cutting off your air supply watching you pass away. However, we were taught to love other people the way we wanted to be loved. So we appreciate the Edomites who stand, shoulder-to-shoulder, with Israelites fighting racial and social injustices for all.

Without the help of some Edomite people, there is a possibility that, Israelites may still be enslaved in this country. The Union soldiers stood up, with their lives, to free Israelites in the Civil War. Today, their descendants are protesting beside us for the senseless killings of Israelite George Floyd and others whom have fallen victim to law enforcement murders. Overzealous police officers with a superiority complex, racial hatred, and a gun have slaughtered over time thousands of Israelites. Fortunately, in today's society we are equipped with cell phones and surveillance cameras to record their carnage.

The Bible promises it won't be like this always. The Lord says the first shall be last and the last shall be first. The head shall be the tail and the tail shall be the head. White supremacists know these scriptures like the back of their hand. They ponder day and night ways to thwart these prophecies from coming to pass. They will lie, cheat, steal, and kill to maintain their authoritarian ways.

Chapter 3

The 400-Year Mark, in Prophecy

As of August 20, 2019, it's been four hundred years since August 20, 1619. It marks the date when the Israelites were first taken captive from their homeland to Jamestown, Virginia, to be afflicted for four hundred years by the nation of Edomites. Prophecy in the Bible states, *"And he said unto Abram, know of a surety that thy seed shall be a stranger in a land that is not theirs, and shall serve them; and they shall afflict them for four hundred years. And also that nation whom they shall serve, will I judge; and afterward shall they come out with great substance"* (Genesis 15:13–14).

Keeping His promise to the Israelites, and well in control, the Lord sent a pandemic worldwide giving all nations of people a reason to bond as one. Prophecy begins to unveil itself on September 18, 2019. The customs office at Wuhan Tianhe Airport received an emergency message that a passenger on an incoming flight was having difficulty breathing. Nine days later, several athletes in China fell ill with flu like symptoms during the Military Games. Not really knowing what the disease was, according to Chinese media, the first Covid-19 case was diagnosed on November 17, 2019. However, five million people had already travelled through Wuhan. It happened before quarantines and before the officials began to seal the borders. Thus, the disease has spread worldwide to one hundred eighty-eight countries killing over 387,634 people in the first seven months of the plague.

Modern-Day Civil Rights Movement

Bible prophecy began further unfolding. The pandemic now has the world economy in a financial crisis. Families have gone for months without income. Unemployment has already reached record highs. People worldwide are frustrated and suffering, trying to get along as nations. Yet, in the midst of the plague, happening on a Monday, May 25, 2020, a Black man, an Israelite George Floyd, was savagely murdered by an Edomite police officer in the United States. With the camera rolling, this took place in front of the whole world, in broad daylight.

The senseless brutal killing of an unarmed subdued man has sparked worldwide protests. Days following Floyd's death national and international protests began. Tens of thousands of people swarmed the streets worldwide. According to Wikipedia, besides the United States, George Floyd's death sparked protests in Auckland, Barcelona, Berlin, Brisbane, Calgary, Copenhagen, Dublin, Lagos, Liberia, Kenya, Ghana, Uganda, Zimbabwe, London, Montreal, Paris, Perth, Rio de Janeiro, Sydney, Tel Aviv, Toronto, Vancouver, Athens, and Thessaloniki.

All the nations of the world began to mourn George Floyd at his first Home Going service held on June 4, 2020, in Minneapolis, Minnesota. It's no coincidence that on the same day, Berlin became the first German state to pass its own Anti-Discrimination

Laws. The next day, on June 5, Washington, DC's, Mayor Muriel Bowser, an Israelite, had "Black Lives Matter" prominently painted on Sixteenth Street leading to the White House and has renamed that section of Sixteenth Street "Black Lives Matter Plaza."

Bible prophecy declares that two thirds of the people on Earth will die. Five months after the four-hundred-year affliction of the Israelites by the Edomites, prophesy was put into motion. The Israelite nation of Blacks, Latino, and Native Americans along with the elderly, began disproportionately dying from a worldwide pandemic known as the Coronavirus. *"And it came to pass, that in all the land said the Lord, two parts therein shall be cut off and die; but the third shall be left therein. And I will bring the third part through the fire, and will refine them as silver is refined, and will try them as gold is tried; they shall call my name, and I will hear them; I will say, it is my people; and they shall say, The Lord is my God"* (Zechariah 13:8).

We must all first understand that the Bible is prophetic. The Prophet Zechariah being in contact with God was able to write about the specific things that will happen in the future, thousands of years ago. The Lord specifically told Zachariah to write that two thirds of the people on Earth shall die, and one third shall remain toward the end of time. *"And this shall be the plague wherewith the Lord shall smite all the people that have fought against Jerusalem: Their flesh shall consume away while they stand upon their feet, and their eyes shall consume away in their holes, and their tongue shall consume away in their mouth"* (Zechariah 14:2).

When I first read this scripture, one of the first things that came to mind was the amplified heat being generated from the sun. The Lord may cause the sun to rotate a little closer to the Earth. Let me ask you a few questions: Besides God moving the sun a little closer to the Earth, what do you think would be powerful enough to melt the flesh off our skin while we are standing upright? What would burn the eyes out of everyone's skull all at once? What would make our tongue consume away from our mouth? Thermal energy from nuclear weapons maybe?

Maybe it is destined by God that mankind will ignite the great heatwave that will ultimately destroy the Earth as we know it. It may be that the missiles are coming. It's possible that in back-to-back launches, a barrage of missiles could be fired simultaneously from many countries, targeting international countries worldwide. From ground to air as well as air-to-air missiles. However, nothing could destroy the Earth faster than God using His sun. Whatever method God chooses to use, prophecy says that the elements shall melt with fervent heat. No one actually knows when, but now everyone knows how. It's going to happen with intense heat and fire. *"But that day of the Lord will come as a thief in the night: in which the heavens shall pass away with a great noise, and the elements shall melt with fervent heat, the earth also and the works that are therein shall be burned up"* (2 Peter 3:10).

The Rapture

However, before the fiery destruction of this old Earth, first comes the Rapture.

Jesus Christ has returned to take all of His children back home with Him. Sounding from the sky were loud angelic voices along with the sound of the trump of God. People worldwide were scared at the sight of Jesus Christ breaking through the clouds. To everyone's surprise, the day of the Rapture has finally arrived. In the blink of an eye, suddenly millions of believers were rising up from the Earth, all at once.

I could see my late parents, grandparents, family as well as friends that had passed away all rising up toward the sky. I'm feeling slightly disoriented as I also begin to rise up in the air toward the clouds. As my feet quickly leave the ground, I begin looking around and about. The last time I looked down things appeared a bit dim, but as far as I can see, people appear to be perplexed and looking up. I heard loud voices of people crying and calling out the names of their loved ones as I was slowly fading away into the distance. I saw all nationalities of other people rising up with me.

Suddenly, I entered into a new dimension, a new state of mind, as I left the atmosphere of this Earth. Then, I could feel my whole body changing into a new body and my mind expanding. I could see the state of things happening on the Earth as well as my family and friends left behind. Car and lane crashes were occurring nationwide. The traffic was at a gridlock worldwide. Emergency responders were helpless due to the traffic. Smoke and fire was everywhere. People worldwide were discombobulated still looking into the sky. People all around the world were still crying for their loved ones. The world is in chaos. Prophesy was being fulfilled.

> *For this we say to you by the word of the Lord, that we which are alive and remain unto the coming of the Lord shall not prevent them which are asleep. For the Lord himself shall descend from heaven with a shout, with the voice of the archangel, and with the trump of God; and the dead in Christ shall rise first. Then we which are alive and remain shall be caught up together with him in*

the clouds, to meet the Lord in the air and so shall we ever be with the Lord. (1 Thessalonians 4:15–17)

The Rapture has now brought about a traumatic change to the world. Many thousands of churches are now in chaos due to the loss of ministers that were taken up in the Rapture. Nations of people are now emotionally devastated due to the sudden loss of their loved ones. There is now a worldwide call for repentance. Due to a new status quo, the world economy soon crashes. Some government officials that had been holding offices in many governmental institutions had been taken up in the Rapture. Numerous presidents across different countries in the world were also taken up in the Rapture, leaving those countries scrambling to find a new president to represent the people of that country.

The Tribulation

The Great Tribulation period is on the horizon. *"For then shall be great tribulation such as not since the beginning of the world to this time, no, nor ever shall be"* (Matthew 24:21). The following are only a few likely scenarios that will take place during the times of the Great Tribulation. Lawlessness is everywhere. International disputes get out of control. Gun sales worldwide will dramatically increase. Due to supply and demand, gun prices would have skyrocketed. A world dictator has risen to power. The New Superpower emerges and establishes an evil Dictatorship Government. With constitutions no longer in effect, the rights of citizens are completely eliminated. The New World Government would be run by violent dictators. Nations of people will be oppressed and have no say so over anything.

Now, false prophets are arising in great numbers all throughout the Earth. Christians are being persecuted and innocent people are being murdered by the tens of thousands. New diseases and plagues will be upon the Earth. Many will try to commit suicide but fail at their every attempt. Satan is working overtime. Brothers will fight against brother. Sisters will kill their own sister. Parents will be attacked by their own children. There will be no allegiance or loyalty to any man, woman, or child. All inhabitants feel betrayed by their loved ones who were caught up in the Rapture. People will become angry and disappointed in who they perceive to be a hateful God.

As it was in the beginning of time, God chose the Israelites to lead the nations of the world to salvation. In the midst of all the madness, at least 144,000 Israelites will be left behind to make that final call for the repentance of sins. God wouldn't just leave nations of people behind with no hope. He is still giving all nations a chance to pay off their debt (sin) through repentance. However, due to the New World Order, coming out of the great tribulation is not going to be easy. *"And I said unto him, Sir, thou know. And he said to me. These are they which came out of the great tribulation, and they have washed their robe, and made them white in the blood of the lamb"* (Revelation 7:14).

In reference to Revelation 7:4–14, the Twelve Tribes of the Children of Israel are the 144,000 that came out of the great tribulation. These one hundred and forty-four thousand Israelites stayed behind after the Rapture to preach the Gospel and the repentance of sins. They were marked by God in their forehead so that no man would try to harm them. Sealed by God, they hungered no more, nor did they thirst. They were filled with the Holy Spirit and God wiped away their tears. They walked all corners of the Earth until every man, woman, and child had a chance to repent and accept Christ as their personal Savior.

Satan was still in charge of the Earth, and his followers would force people to denounce God or be dismembered and tortured. Lucifer came out of the shadows. Satan was bold about being the leader of the New World Order. His minions took leadership of the Earth. No one could buy or sell without the mark of the Beast. Refusal of the mark was, cruelly and painfully, punishable under the new laws. Satan's soldiers would accost and force the mark upon many. Some people are refusing to denounce Jesus Christ and are faithful till death knowing they will receive the crown of life. People to avoid the mark fled to the wilderness and went into hiding, forming tribes for safety.

The dreadful disposition of the world after the Rapture is the constant reminder, to the lost, that the time is at hand. The false prophets throughout the world are teaching many false doctrines. Repentance is heavily on the minds of the lost. Even though knowing that salvation comes only through grace, the only escape from all the chaos that surrounds the people left behind is trying to do what's right in the eyes of God. Out of desperation and fear, people are now trying to work their way into Heaven.

However, they are constantly being reminded by the Children of Israel that all their righteousness in God's sight is nothing but filthy rags. No man is worthy to be saved by his works or supplication. Salvation is a gift bestowed unto Christians who are born again. The acceptance of Christ, sincere repentance, and refusing the mark are the only messages taught by the Twelve Tribes of Israel throughout the world.

More difficult days are looming over the horizon. According to prophecy, these are a few more scenarios that will take place during the times of the great tribulation. The remaining Israelites with the mark of God in their foreheads will have all the powers Jesus Christ demonstrated while He was on the Earth. In addition, they will have the power to turn waters into blood, stop the rain and smite the Earth with plagues. The very mouth of the sealed Israelites will become as weapons. Fire will proceed out of their mouths, and they will devour their enemies.

The plot thickens when powerful and destructive earthquakes, along with erupting volcanoes, start happening very frequently throughout the world. Earthquakes that register high on the Richter scale can effect things like the power grids, toppling of buildings, highways, and roads upheaval, etc. Volcanoes whose lava consumes acres of land with hot molten fire will destroy everything in its path, along with its ash blackening and polluting the sky. Famine will run rabid all over the world. On any given day, the Bible says that the sun will lose its light and go dark.

From previous earthquakes the power grids have already been compromised. No electricity or sunlight leads to more lawlessness. The moon will turn to blood. To see the moon being turned to blood is all-out horrifying. Many stars all at once will suddenly plummet from space killing thousands while making large craters upon the Earth. A star will fall into the waters on Earth contaminating the waters, and many people will die because of the contaminated waters.

There will come a time when hail and fire mingled with blood will fall from the sky, setting all of Earth's green grass on fire as well as one third of its trees. Four angels will be given one year, one day, and one hour to slay one third of all men that are still living on the Earth. Mountains will be moved from their places. The people that never repented from their murders, thefts, fornication, and abominations shall remain and attempt to hide themselves. However, there is nowhere to hide.

Signs of the End-Times

The false prophets of deception is one of the primary signs of the end-times. The Bible states that many will come forward claiming to be the Second Coming. False prophets can be found everywhere in the year 2020 from televangelist in mega churches to the presidency. On August 21, 2019, multibillionaire and current president of the United States, Donald J. Trump, touted himself as the King of Israel, the Chosen One.

There are going to be wars and rumors of wars. The countries that are presently at war are Nigeria, South Sudan, Ukraine, Iraq, Syria, Somalia, Yemen, Afghanistan, and many others. Rumored are tensions between the US and China, Saudi Arabia, and civil unrest in the United States. American households are warring against themselves with parents killing their own children, brother against brother, and children in opposition to their parents.

There will be more natural disasters. The Earth has taken a turn for the worst. We know that global warming is increasing the Earth's average temperature and rapidly heating up the Earth's climate system. Due to the Earth's overheating, its glaciers are melting at record rates. Acts of God such as wildfires are raging out of control, killing residents, demolishing land, and devouring wildlife.

Within the first six months of the year 2020, there has been over 19,000 wildfires recorded worldwide burning over 400,000 acres of land. There were more wildfires in the UK in 2019 than ever recorded in history. Ten major tsunamis are occurring every hundred years. The Indian Ocean tsunami of 2004 killed over 235,000 people. Also the frequent occurrence, high death rate and destruction caused by hurricanes, tornadoes, floods, snowstorms, blizzards, earthquakes, and erupting volcanoes across the globe are prominent signs of the end-times.

Emerging infectious diseases are also signs of the end-times. As global warming quickly heats up the Earth, the warm temperatures allow diseases to transmit easier and rapidly spread through the air we breathe. These diseases spread through atmospheric circulation of air, from person to person, in close contact. The Coronavirus is the newest pandemic spreading the globe killing by the thousands. Other diseases such as swine flu, SARS, MERS, Ebola, and AIDS emerged within the last forty years.

Different cancers are transmitted to the Israelites from foods that God forbids us to eat—foods such as swine and seafood without scales and fins. As we approach the end-times, new diseases without vaccines will become more prevalent.

The Gospel of Jesus Christ being preached worldwide is another prominent sign of the second coming. Radio and television are instrumental in declaring and spreading the Gospel. Another way that the Gospel is being declared to the nations around the world is through evangelism. Many people spend their whole lives reaching people through missionary work. In addition to that, today's technologies of television, computers, cell phones, and satellites allow the Gospel to be preached in every part of the globe.

The Bible declares that the poor will always be with us. Famine is nothing new. It is prevalent in places like South Sudan and Ethiopia. In many other countries like Zambia, Uganda, and Yemen, people are starving to death. Even in the US, one in six children go to bed hungry, and the long list goes on and on. Throughout these regions, malnutrition and pestilences has already taken its toll on many millions of lives. However, as we approach these last days, food and water insecurities worldwide will start creating political and social unrest. According to prophecy, our present state of famine and pestilences here in America is a cool walk in the park in comparison to the prevalence of the end-times.

Hope for All Mankind

The Lord was deeply disappointed when He said, "I repent that I have made man." This is the only regret of God in the Bible. It's like the Lord saying, "I apologize that I have made an image of myself to be represented by people whom I have created on the Earth." He felt remorse because His Image that He had created to live on the Earth was not representing the Holy and sinless nature of Himself in Heaven. God created us in His image to represent who He is.

I can't see how anyone, by any stretch of the imagination, could fail to understand why God felt remorse over how mankind represented His image. When you look in the mirror you see an image of yourself. Not an image of someone you don't know or recognize. If I looked in the mirror and saw an image of someone other than myself, frankly, I don't know what I would do because a mirror should reflect my image. When you gaze into the mirror, you should see God since you were created in His image. *"So God created man in his own image, in the image of God created he him; male and female created he them"* (Genesis 1:27).

God was so disappointed in us, as sinners, that He pondered eliminating us as a species. If it wasn't for the empathy of His Son, no life would exist today on Earth. Jesus, in his great mercy and wisdom, volunteered to walk amongst us to prove we could be saved by His blood, giving us a chance to be adopted by God, and become brothers and sisters to Jesus, changing God's perception of us. Now, when God looks at us, He sees Himself again instead of our flaws and iniquities.

What a sacrifice God made for mankind. He permitted His only Son and best friend, who had been with Him from the beginning, to leave His side and serve the nations of the world. The Father, the Son, and The Holy Spirit had been constant companions. Now, for the sake of mankind, Jesus and the great Comforter subjected themselves to leaving Heaven and descending to the Earth. Through the Holy Trinity, Jesus's life on Earth was predestined and ordained. He gave His life so that we could have everlasting lives in Heaven.

Hope for all mankind emerges with the physical birth of Jesus in Bethlehem of Judea. The child grew in strength and wisdom in the city of Nazareth. At the age of twelve, He snuck off and started preaching in a Jerusalem temple. When the twelve-year-old Jesus spoke, the doctors along with everyone else in the temple were amazed at His knowledge and understanding. His parents, Joseph and Mary, had been looking for Jesus for three days. When they finally caught up with Jesus preaching in the temple, they asked Him where He had been. Jesus responded as such: "What do you mean, where have I been? Didn't you know that I must be about my Father's business?"

From the age of thirteen until the age of twenty-nine, the Bible mentions nothing about the life Jesus lived except that He worked as a carpenter in the village of Nazareth. At the age of thirty, He started His public ministry in Northern Galilee located in Northern Israel. The first subject matter Jesus preached in Galilee was to repent and believe in the Gospel, giving the people hope. As the people hung on to every word of Jesus, the good news would give them reassurance and a sense of purpose and hope.

Jesus Performed Miracles

Jesus turns water into wine. The Lord's first public miracle was the changing of water into wine at the request of His mother at a wedding in Cana of Galilee. The sight of water being turned into wine right before their very eyes astonished the attendees. When the master of the house ran out of wine, Mary asked Jesus to create more. This was a test of obedience. As He turned pitchers of water into wine, people who didn't witness the miracle thought the master had saved the best wine for last.

Five of His Disciples were at the wedding. Watching Jesus perform the great miracle confirmed to them that they should continue to follow Him.

Jesus feeding five thousand people. In Tabgha, Capernaum on the northwest shore of the Sea of Galilee, thousands of people had followed Him to hear Him speak. Some had traveled from faraway lands, and Jesus knew it would be cruel to send them home hungry. He had His Disciples bring to Him what food they could find. They presented Him with two fish and five loaves of bread. Jesus blessed the food and told them to pass it out among the hungry. That two fish and five loaves of bread multiplied to feed five thousand. This was not the only account of Jesus feeding thousands. According to the Gospels of Mark and Matthew, Jesus fed four thousand followers with two fish and seven loaves of bread.

Catching the great multitude of fish. While Jesus was preaching near the Sea of Galilee, He saw two boats at the water's edge. He boarded the boat belonging to Simon and began to preach. When He learned that Simon had only caught a few fish all day, He told him to sail the boat back into the waters and to cast the net over the right side of the boat. He did as Jesus instructed. When Simon pulled in the net, he had captured a great multitude of fish—more than ever before. Simon was amazed and asked, "What manner of a man was this?" Jesus answered and said, "Follow Me and I will make you a fisher of men." From that day forward, Simon's name was changed to Peter and he loyally followed Jesus.

Jesus walked on the waters of the sea. It came to pass after Jesus fed the five thousand, He sent His disciples by ship to the other side of the Sea of Galilee while He stayed behind to pray. According to the Gospels of Matthew, Mark, John, and Luke, they saw Jesus walk on the Sea of Galilee across the waters to the ship. His Disciples thought they were seeing a ghost. When He entered the ship the rough waters and wind became calm, and His Disciples knew that they were witnessing something special.

Jesus raises Lazarus from the dead. Mary and Martha sent word out to Jesus that their brother Lazarus was sick. His sisters knew that Jesus would want to heal His best friend, but their pleas for Jesus's return came too late, and Lazarus died. When Jesus arrived four days after Lazarus had died, Mary and Martha told Jesus that He was too late. Jesus insisted that his sisters take Him to where Lazarus was entombed. Jesus prayed over His best friend and Lazarus arose as if he had never been sick.

Jesus raises Jairus's daughter from the dead. Jairus, one of the rulers of the synagogue, had sought out Jesus to heal his twelve-year-old daughter. As they traveled to Jairus's house, a woman who had bleeding issues touched Jesus's garment, and was instantly healed. Before they could get to Jairus's home, they were informed that his daughter had died. Jesus continued to his house because He knew He could still help her. Jesus only allowed Peter, James, and John to follow Him into the house where Jairus's daughter lay dead. The other people in the house cried and mourned the daughter's loss. When Jesus asked them to take Him to the daughter, they mocked and laughed at Him and said He was too late. That's when the Lord put everyone out the house except the mother, father, and His

Disciples. Then Jesus took the girl's hand and told her to arise, and right away the girl arose and walked.

Jesus raises the son of a widow from the dead. In the village of Nain, two miles south of Mount Tabor, Jesus, His Disciples, and a huge crowd came across a funeral procession. The Lord followed them to the burial site. A widow was mourning the loss of her only son. Jesus approached her and comforted the widow. Then He went up and touched the bier they were carrying her son on. The son of the widow immediately sat up and started talking. Word of this miracle spread all throughout the land.

The exorcism of a young man. A young man was brought to Jesus with epileptic symptoms. He was foaming at the mouth, grinding his teeth, and his body was as rigid as a board. The boy's father had asked Jesus's Disciples to heal his son, but they were unable to do so. When the man brought his son to Jesus, He said it was from lack of faith that no one else was able to heal him. Jesus asked the man if he believed He could heal him. The man responded, "Yes," that he believed. Then the Lord commanded the spirit to leave the young man, and He helped him from the ground. He was completely healed.

Jesus heals and exorcises many. After Jesus healed Peter's mother-in-law, word went out in all the land that a great Prophet had come. The Lord was bombarded with sick and possessed people. Jesus exorcised many evil spirits with a word and healed the sick. He also encountered one demonic spirit that called himself Legion, for he was many. When Jesus confronted Legion, he asked that he be able to go into a herd of swine. Jesus complied and caused the swine to run into a lake and drown themselves.

Jesus gives sight to Bartimaeus. As Jesus approached Jericho, a blind man sat by the roadside begging. He heard the crowd passing by and asked what was happening. They told him Jesus was coming through. The blind beggar began to cry out. "Jesus, Son of David, have mercy on me!" The crowd shushed him, but he yelled even louder. Jesus heard his cries and had the beggar brought to Him. He asked him what he wanted. The man asked that his sight be restored. Jesus responded, "Your faith has made you well." Bartimaeus immediately regained his sight and followed Jesus glorifying God as all the people saw the healing.

Jesus heals the blind by spitting into his eyes. Jesus and His Disciples entered into Bethsaida, on the north shore of Galilee. A blind man was brought to the Lord and they asked Him to touch him. Instead, Jesus led the man to the outskirts of town, and when they were alone, He spit on his eyes and laid hands on him. The man looked up and said he did not see clearly. The Lord then put His hands upon his eyes and made him look up again and his vision was restored completely. Jesus sent him away to his house and told him not to tell anyone.

Jesus healed the man that was born blind. The Lord came upon a man that was born blind. His Disciples inquired why a man would be born blind. They wondered aloud to Jesus whose sin caused the man to be born blind. They asked if the parents of the blind man had sinned or did the blind man sin to cause him to be born that way. The Lord informed them that neither had sinned. He was born blind so that Jesus could heal him and glorify the Father which is in Heaven. Jesus spit on the ground and made clay out of his spittle. Then He anointed the eyes of the blind man with the clay. Jesus instructed the man to wash in the pool of Siloam. The man went and washed and his sight was fully restored.

Jesus healed the leper. Great multitudes of people followed Jesus and His Disciples. He healed the sick and cast out demons everywhere He went. On this day, a leper came to Him and worshipped Him. The leper asked that he be cleansed if it be Jesus's will. The Lord reached out His hand and touched the leper and ordered him to be clean, and immediately, his leprosy was gone. Jesus ordered him to show himself to the priest and offer the gift that Moses commanded for a testimony unto them.

Jesus healed a paralytic man. When Jesus was living in Capernaum, teaching and preaching to His followers, there were so many people gathered that no one else could get into the house. Some men came with a paralyzed man, but since it was too crowded for them to get into the door, they created an opening in the roof and lowered the man sick of the palsy in front of Jesus. The Lord was so impressed by their faith that He said, "Son, be of good cheer; thy sins be forgiven thee." And he was healed.

Jesus heals a paralytic man at the pool of Bethesda. The Lord went to Jerusalem by the healing pool of Bethesda. He came upon a man who had been paralyzed for thirty-eight years. The pool had five porches and in these, laid many sick people. Jesus asked the paralyzed man if he wished to be healed. The man responded that he did, but he had no one to help him into the water. Jesus took mercy upon him and said, "Rise, take up thy bed and walk." And straightaway, the man was made whole.

These are some of the supernatural events Jesus performed while He walked the Earth. He held all power in His hands. Jesus so loved mankind that He forbad not anybody that needed His holy touch. Often, He asked that His works be kept secret, but the healed couldn't keep the fact that Jesus had blessed them to themselves. He and His many Disciples worked miracles and wonders making believers out of doubters and giving hope to the world.

Chapter 4

Crucifixion of Jesus

Hope for all the nations of the world was embodied in the death, entombment, and resurrection of Jesus Christ. However, to the Roman soldiers, the purpose of having the Lord crucified was to destroy His reputation and popularity He had built for himself over the span of three years. The carpenter's son proclaiming to be King of the Jews was seen as an insult to many of the people. This gave them a reason to want Him killed. They pondered a way to take Him captive. Many of the people in the city remembered the countless miracles that Jesus had performed, which brought Him much respect and admiration. Others were envious and jealous because they could not perform miracles. They began to plot a legal way to have Jesus killed.

After some pondering the chief priests remembered that Jesus would be teaching in the temple and the next day would be the Passover. The timing was perfect, so they constructed the perfect plan. With the help of Satan and Judas Iscariot, one of the Twelve Disciples, they figured out a way he could make some money. That's when he decided he could sell out Jesus in order to line his pockets with silver. He went to the chief priests and outlined his plan of betrayal.

It was time for the Passover, so Judas joined Jesus and the eleven other Disciples for the last supper. While dining with them, Jesus informed them that He knew that one of them would betray Him. After eating and drinking, Judas left to find the chief priests so he could deliver Jesus into their hands and collect his spending money—thirty pieces of silver, as prophesied. Soon after, the Lord also left and went out to Mount of Olives, followed by His other Disciples. Arriving at the Garden of Gethsemane, Jesus kneeled down and prayed to the Father. After He prayed, here came Judas and several soldiers walking toward Him.

When Judas got close enough, he kissed Jesus. The Lord then replied, "You betrayed me." That's when Peter drew his sword and cut off one of the soldier's right ear. When that happened, Jesus touched the soldier's ear, and another jaw-dropping miracle was performed by Jesus—his ear was restored. However, the miracle did not stop the soldiers from capturing Jesus and taking Him away to kill Him.

The soldiers took Jesus to court, and the chief priests interrogated Him with the question, "Are you Christ?" Jesus responded, "If I tell you the truth, you won't believe me. Neither will you let me go." They continued to interrogate Christ with the same old question. Jesus responded, "You said that I am the Son of God." That really upset them! Pilate asked Jesus if he was King of the Jews. Jesus responded, "You said it…" Proclaiming Jesus to be innocent, Pilate turned Jesus over to Herod's jurisdiction. Christ did not want to talk to Herod. Neither did He respond when Herod questioned Him. So Herod and his men mocked Jesus, put a nice robe on Him, and sent Him back to Pilate.

Finding no fault in Jesus, Pilate was willing to release Him. However, the crowd of people screamed out, saying, "Crucify Him!" Pilate said, for the third time, he found no cause to kill Him, but the loud voices of the chief priests and the crowd prevailed. So Pilate let the people do whatever they wanted to do with Christ, which was crucify Him. The soldiers then began to spit on Jesus as they mocked Him. The soldiers were so bent on social indignation and public humiliation that the higher purpose of the crucifixion (the penalty for sins) never really crossed their minds.

While they had Jesus in the common hall, they continued to mock Him. They stripped Him of His clothes and put a scarlet robe on Him. Then, a few overexcited solders went outside looking for thorns to inflict more pain on Jesus. They carefully gathered thorns from a nearby bush and cautiously pleated them into a make-believe crown, for the purpose of mocking Jesus. After coming back inside, they carefully placed the crown of thorns on Jesus's head, avoiding sticking themselves with the thorns.

Just for fun, they gave Jesus a reed and bowed in front of Him. With sarcasm in their voices, they were screaming, "King of the Jews!" First, they spit on Him. Next, they gave Him thirty-nine lashes (which, ironically, equals one for each book in the Old Testament). Then, they took the reed and hit Jesus on the head with it, pushing thorns into his skin, causing Him to bleed. Afterward, they stripped Him of the scarlet robe, returned His clothes to Him, and took Him to Golgotha for the crucifixion.

At nine in the morning, the solders hung Jesus on the cross between two other men being crucified. Still playing around, the chief priests along with elders would mock Jesus saying, "If you are God's Son, save yourself and come down from the cross." Around noon, Jesus cried out with a loud voice, and they continued to mock Him. After three more grueling hours of pain, Jesus cried out once more, hung His head and died. At that moment, a great earthquake shook the ground where they were standing.

Resurrection

After the burial and the Sabbath, on the dawn of the first day of the week, another earthquake came and shook the ground in Jerusalem. That's when an angel descended from Heaven and rolled back the stone from Christ's grave and sat upon it. The face of the angel was as bright as lightning, and his robe was white like snow. The greatest of all miracles was the resurrection of Jesus Christ from the dead. Now, having a new and glorified body, Jesus was able to appear and disappear suddenly. *"And their eyes were opened, and they knew him; and he vanished out of their sight"* (Luke 24:31).

After the resurrection Mary Magdalene came to the tomb crying and looking for Jesus. As she kneeled down, she observed two angels sitting where Jesus had been laid to rest. After speaking with the angels, she turned around and there stood Jesus. She didn't recognize Him at first, but when Jesus called out her name, she knew it was Him. They spoke briefly. Afterwards, Mary went to the Disciples and told them that Jesus had risen from the dead. The same evening as the Disciples, except for Thomas, were sitting and talking with the door closed, Jesus came and appeared and stood in the midst of them. They were astonished and filled with joy. When the Disciples encountered Thomas, they were excited and told him that Jesus had risen from the dead. However, Thomas did not believe them.

Eight days later when all the Disciples were together, with the door closed again, Jesus appeared and stood in the midst of them. Speaking directly to Thomas, Jesus said, "Put your finger in the nail print of my hand. Put your hand into my wounded side. Now… do you believe?" His doubting Disciple cried out: "My Lord! My God!" Thomas believed because he saw Jesus the Christ for himself. Jesus admonished Thomas. Christ then said, "It is wonderful that you now believe, but it is more blessed that you see me not… and yet believe."

Jesus Returns Back to the Father

The Lord appeared unto Simon Peter, Thomas, and two more of the Disciples for the third and last time after the resurrection to perform a miracle and dine with them before he ascended back home to The Father. Peter, Thomas, and the other Disciples had been fishing all night but caught nothing. When the next morning arrived, they looked out and saw a man standing on the shore, not knowing at first that it was Jesus. So the Lord asked them if they had caught anything, and they responded, "No." However, they knew His voice. Jesus told them to cast the net on the right side of the ship, and that's what they did. After doing so, they pulled out a multitude of fish. One hundred and fifty-three, to be exact.

After dining with his Disciples, Jesus asked Peter, on three separate occasions, if he loved Him. Peter replied, "Yes, Lord," each time. That's when Jesus replied, saying, "Feed my sheep," and again He said, "Feed my lambs." As the conversation drew to an end, Jesus commanded them not to leave Jerusalem. Instead, to wait until they receive the power of the Holy Spirit. Once they receive the Holy Spirit, then they would be able to witness worldwide.

After this final conversation with the Disciples, Jesus quickly ascended up toward the clouds and disappeared out of sight. As the Disciples stood there, gazing into the clouds, two men appeared standing next to them dressed in white. These two men spoke to the Disciples and told them that the same Jesus will return in the clouds in the same like manner that He left. The Disciples rejoiced and vowed to spend their lives teaching and preaching the life, death, and resurrection of their beloved friend and leader.

The Comforter Arrives on Earth

The promise prevails. Jesus had previously warned His Disciples before His crucifixion that the time would soon come when they would not see Him anymore. He told them that it was vital that He go away to the Father, in order that He could send the Holy Spirit of Truth, the Comforter, back to them. Jesus informed His Disciples that they would need the Comforter because the world didn't believe He was the Son of God. The Holy Spirit that Christ sent to them would help guide them teach and reprove the world of sin.

It was the Day of Pentecost. Eager anticipation of the coming of the Comforter was upon each Disciple as they were gathered together on one accord. People of different nationalities that spoke different languages were gathered and attending the Pentecost festival in Jerusalem with the Disciples. As the powerful sound of a mighty wind entered into the room where the Disciples were sitting, the Holy Spirit descended upon the Apostles. The intercession between the Disciples and The Holy Spirit materialized as promised. That's when, suddenly, all the Apostles began speaking in tongues, glorifying Christ.

With great authority, the Spirit Counselor in each of them began teaching the Gospel in various languages. From different nations, the great multitude of people were native Arabians, Cretans, Parthians, Medes, Elamites, Mesopotamians, Cappadocians, Pontians, and Asians. Also from Phrygia, Pamphylia, Egypt, Libya, Cyrene, Rome; Jews and Proselytes. As the multitude of people listened to the Apostles speak the

Gospel of Christ in their native tongues, they were all amazed at their sayings and many began to believe. Others mocked them accusing them of being drunk. Apostle Peter stood up for the other Disciples letting the crowd of people know that they were not intoxicated, but filled with the Holy Spirit.

When the third hour had passed, Peter began to preach the Gospel. He convinced the multitude that they were sinners in need of salvation from sin. He spoke of things that were spoken by the Prophet Joel, concerning prophecy. Then the Apostle Peter began prophesying himself. He also spoke of things concerning King David. Then Peter brought to their attention the crucifixion and resurrection of Jesus Christ. Finally, he relayed the Gospel's message to repent, believe, and be baptized in the name of Jesus. By the end of the day, three thousand souls were added to the church, and the Church of Christ grew rapidly.

Hostility Aimed at God

The raging hostility of the oppressors against the Israelites isn't based upon the color of their skin. Rather, it is based upon the Nation of Israelites being God's chosen people. The animosity of the Edomites against God in Heaven is the key to understanding the problems of racial inequality, injustice, and social indignation here on Earth. The inability of the oppressor to hurt and kill the Father in Heaven causes the oppressor to hurt and kill His Israelite children here on Earth. By understanding the opposition against God's choice, you understand the world conspiracy of the Edomites against the Israelites.

One hand washes the other. Just as God the Father did not choose the Nation of Edomites as His chosen people; neither did His Son, Jesus Christ, choose Edomites as His Twelve Disciples. Like Father. Like Son. The Father chose the twelve sons of Jacob to become the twelve Tribes of Israel, and the Son would choose twelve Hebrew Israelites to be His followers. Jesus cautioned His disciples that they would be hated, because the world first hated Him.

Get the picture now? The hatred and hostility runs deep. This is why Israelites are cruelly mistreated and do not receive the same privileges as the Edomites. They don't directly hate you. They hate the Father and the Son in Heaven for choosing the Israelites to be the nation above all nations on the Earth. *"For thou art an holy people unto the Lord thy God, and the Lord hath chosen thee to be a peculiar people unto himself, above all the nations that are upon the earth"* (Deuteronomy 14:2).

With the support of the United States government, Israelites, especially the Native Americans and Black Jews, are hunted down in the streets and killed. With the Roman government on the shoulders of the Black Jew, Jesus Christ, He was hunted down and brutally crucified. All except for one of the Disciples whom Jesus truly loved were brutally murdered as well. The Roman government set the stage for the suicide death of the Lord's Disciple Judas Iscariot, who was racked with guilt after betraying Jesus.

God's chosen people, the Israelites, since the beginning, were targeted for extermination by the Edomites. Like the Blacks in today's society, all Twelve Disciples chosen by Jesus Christ were hated, hunted down, and legally killed like animals. Both Disciples, Simon Peter and Andrew, were crucified on the cross, painfully hung upside down until they died. The Apostle James had an instant death as he was inhumanely beheaded. The Apostle Phillip was nailed to a cross. The Disciple Bartholomew was mercilessly skinned alive then beheaded. The Apostle Matthew was burned to death. The Apostle James was stoned to death. Both Disciples Simon and Jude were sawed and axed to death. Saint John was thrown into boiling oil and yet survived. Apostle Thomas was stabbed to death with a spear. Finally, Matthias, the last Apostle, was stoned to death, then beheaded.

Their fate, like Jesus before them, was sealed by their convictions and teachings. In their day, Christianity was considered heresy and disrespectful to the scribes. They gave their lives rather than denounce what they knew to be true. They preached to anyone who would listen. Christ lived, died, and was resurrected so we might all have a chance at everlasting life. It is because of their obedience and sacrifices that we know of Jesus Christ today. The first stories of Jesus were recorded in the scriptures within fifty years of His death and the validity of His life has been verified by many witnesses.

Life in Arsareth/America— Spiritual Egypt

America is the modern-day Spiritual Egypt. Being shipped out to the land of Egypt, the Israelites were stripped of their culture as well as their rights all because they disobeyed God. The Lord's plan is to set the Nation of Israelites above all other nations on the Earth. According to the Bible, God will succeed, and the Israelites will be set above all other nations on Earth. You can bank on that.

Here's how we got where we are today. Our Patriarch Abraham was born in the city of Ur in Mesopotamia. He first arrived at the shore of Jordan, searching for the

Promised Land beyond the horizon of the desert. Their pilgrimage in the desert was originally meant to last forty days, but the Children of Israel complained constantly before God. Because they murmured before the Lord, now they had to wander in the wilderness for forty years.

After wandering in the desert for forty years, only their children survived and reached the Promised Land of Canaan. The rest of the congregation perished on the way in the wilderness. So we, the Israelites, made it to the Promised Land of Canaan. However, after we got there, we became a sinful nation of people. Remember, we are God's chosen people and His laws were given to us to obey.

Here we go again, not wanting to joyfully serve the Lord and keep His commandments. He already knows what's best for us! Because of disobedience our testing periods went from forty days to forty years to four hundred years. When will we learn? *"And God spoke on the wise that his seed should sojourn in a strange land; and that they should bring them into bondage, and entreat them evil four hundred years. And the nation to whom they shall be in bondage will I judge said God: and after that shall they come forth, and serve me in this place"* (Acts 7:6–7). Captured and transported away from our natural homeland to here, we are now living in the United States.

Living here in Arsareth/America under the rule of the Edomites, the Israelites can no longer experience the richness in their own land, as well as their own culture. The Israelites had established their own political system. They were accustomed to having and operating their own social institutions. Israelites were innovators. They created paper and were the first architects. Always having a great passion for building, they created the mathematical formulas needed for the construction of pyramids and built them. The Israelites were doctors and scientists creating their own medicines.

Before being kidnapped and taken away from their thousands of acres of rich land, their income had revolved mainly around their flocks and herds of animals. With the new status quo in a strange land, being taken away, the Israelites no longer had the option of tilling their own land. They could no longer take pride in supplying their own basic needs of food, water, clothing, and shelter. Neither could they take care of their own families. Hence, enslaved Israelites had to depend on Edomites for all their basic needs.

Living in their homeland, the Israelites took pride in taking care and had a deep appreciation and love for their family. Being kidnapped, their spirits were broken by the permanent separation of husbands from wives, and sisters from brothers. The young girls and women were sexually abused in transit. The males demoralized by Edomite men on the ships, while they were being transported to America. Upon arrival, families were separated to be sold into slavery. Many of the families would never see their relatives again.

Israelites living in the US—rich or poor—believing that they have been freed from slavery are only fooling themselves. Black Jews and Israelites are legally treated like animals in today's society. Israelites living in America are economic slaves. The Edomites will never tell you. Neither do they want you to have enough sense to figure it out. You are enslaved by their system. When you have to go to a different nation of people for all your basic necessities, you are enslaved. Which nation of people are collecting money from the Israelites to feed their families? Are the Israelites manufacturing their own foods? The truth is, being free in our homeland, we were growing our own food, to feed our own families.

Oh, so you own your own business. Okay, so which nation of people are you forced to pay your taxes to? Which nation of people are you forced to pay money in order to receive the permits needed to operate your business? Which nation of people do you pay for electricity? It's not the Nation of Israelites. Which nation of people own the water systems here in the United States? No one can live without water. The Israelites have to go to another nation of people to drink water. They have to pay the Edomites the wages they earn to supply our families with food, shelter and clothing.

God said that in His time, He will set the Nation of Israelites above all nations upon the Earth. That's when all other nations on Earth will be paying their property and sales taxes to the Israelites. The Edomites will never tell the Israelites that their social security numbers are actually their slave numbers here in America. Blacks were never meant to and will never become true citizens in the US.

They never tell you that Edomites pay their taxes to their own people. If by chance you live long enough to see your retirement age, who will control and distribute your forty-four years of monthly Social Security checks?

By the way, the system is set up so that over 90 percent of the Israelites in the US die long before their hard-earned retirement money is paid out to them. Therefore, the Edomites over the years has banked countless billions of unpaid retirement dollars earned by the Israelites living in America. These billions of dollars collected from the dead Israelites' retirement funds are being spent by the United States government to this day. Death is an annual multibillion dollar industry to the US government. Yet, most families have to suffer financially to bury their dead. For the Israelites, that's just life in the American Spiritual Egypt.

Cultural Copycats

The Israelites became the cultural copycats of the Edomite culture. As a child living in Houston, Texas, coming up in the 1960s, light-skinned Black children in my classrooms would make fun of dark-skinned people. The books we learned from in the '60s defined the color black as always being negative. On the other hand, the definition of the color white was always something positive. The word *black* would mean ugly, nasty, and dirty while the word *white* meant purity and cleanliness. Therefore, going by what we had learned as children, we were ashamed because we were called Black.

Not knowing what represented true beauty, Black people became ashamed of their wooly hair as well as their dark skin. If the Creator wanted the Black Jew Israelites to have straight hair and lighter skin, He would have created them with it. Keep in mind that we were created in the image of God. Wooly hair and dark skin on Black Israelites was created for God to enjoy. He is the creator of beauty. His only begotten Son, Jesus Christ, the King of the Jews, had dark skin and wooly hair. Created to represent His Father in Heaven, who could be more beautiful than Him?

    However, to fit in and please our oppressors, Black men and women shunned themselves by bleaching their skin for lighter skin tones. After bleaching their skin, the wooly haired Israelite men and women began putting perms in their hair to straighten it. They saw wooly hair as being ugly and straight hair as being beautiful. *"Envy not the oppressor and choose none of his ways"* (Psalm 3:31). The Israelites, over time, joined the Edomites in their festivities and adapted their culture of eating unclean foods. Not only eating and drinking with the Edomites, feeling free, the Israelites also saw them as husbands and wives.

    They have now embraced the Stockholm syndrome. The Israelite nation of men and women would fall in love with their captives the Edomites. They would marry and have children with Edomites, adulterating the Israelite Nation of people. The cultural practice is known as interracial marriage. According to the word of *Apocrypha, King James Version,* "Beware of all whoredom, *my son, and chiefly take a wife of the seed of thy father, and take not a strange woman to wife, which is not of thy father's tribe; for we are the children of the prophets, Noel, Abraham, Isaac and Jacob; remember my son that our fathers from the beginning, even that they all married wives of their own kindred, and were blessed in their children, and their seed shall inherit the land"* (Tobit 4:12).

Celebrating God's Holidays

Before the Israelites were captured and taken from their homeland, they were accustomed to celebrating the Lord's holidays. Praising God had always been the focus of their daily lives. The seven Holy holidays were the Sabbath day, Passover, the Feast of Unleavened Bread, the Day of Pentecost, Day of Atonement, Feast of the Trumpets, and the Feast of Tabernacles. However, after the Israelites were freed from slavery, the Americans enticed the Israelites with their pagan festivals. As time went on, the Israelites began to participate in their culture by celebrating pagan holidays that boost the United States economy, namely, birthdays, New Year's, Valentine's, St. Patrick's, Easter, Thanksgiving, Halloween, and Christmas.

Anytime Israelites celebrate pagan holidays that were set up by man and forsake the holidays established by God, they bring curses upon themselves. Let's talk about the Sabbath Day. Before the Father created the Israelites, He knew that they were created to work hard and build the structures throughout the Earth. So for the sake of our physical and mental health, God specifically commands the Israelites (Exodus 31:16–17) to rest on the seventh day of every week. Because the Lord rested on the seventh day, He was refreshed. Israelites must obey and represent the Covenant of God because being created in His image, we are to represent Him.

The Day of Atonement. Like the Sabbath, (Leviticus 16:26–30), the Lord commands another day of rest. It's another great day worth celebrating. On this holiday, we celebrate the Son of God. The Day of Atonement represents the day that Jesus Christ took away the sins of the world by way of His death on the cross. He died for the sins and salvation of all the nations across the globe.

Look forward to celebrating The Lord's Passover. According to the Bible (Leviticus 23:5), beginning in the evening of the first month and the fourteenth day is the Lord's Passover. The holiday represents the events that surrounds the tenth plague. By remembering where you came from, you can have a better vision of where you are going. Therefore, celebrate the Emancipation Day of the Israelites from slavery under the Egyptians. It represents the day that God passed over the houses of the Israelites whom had marked their doorpost with blood as He commanded. He punished the Egyptians by killing all of their first-born children and the first-born animals per household that day. What an event to be remembered.

Taking place annually, the Feast of Unleavened Bread becomes one continuous festival with the Passover. Lasting for seven days, this holiday celebrates the Lord, bringing the Israelites out of slavery in the land of Egypt. The Lord commands us to observe the celebration (Leviticus

12:17–18) throughout all the generations of the Israelites.

The Day of Pentecost commemorates the day the Holy Spirit came upon the Disciples after Jesus ascended back to the Father. It represents the birthday of the Church. This Christian Festival is to be celebrated annually on the seventh Sunday after Easter. It's a day to remember and celebrate the Comforter. Jesus promised the Disciples that He would send them an Intercessor to be with them. That Comforter is known as the Holy Spirit.

Celebrating the protection of the Father. The Feast of Tabernacles is celebrated annually (Numbers 29:12) for seven days. The festival celebrates God protecting the Israelites as they wandered in the wilderness of the desert for forty years. Happening at harvest time, the Israelites would build themselves shelters to live in for seven days, eating and drinking, remembering how God brought them out of the land of Egypt and ending them being enslaved to the Egyptians.

Mark your calendar for God's holiday known as the Feast of the Trumpets. This festival represents another Sabbath day of rest and convocation (Leviticus 23:24). The feast of trumpets represents the blowing of the trumpets of God. The sounding of the trumpets sounds the alarm for the dire need of the repentance of sins. It's also a day that God sets aside for His people to come together and reflect on the seven angels preparing to sound the seven trumpets announcing the final seven plagues on the Earth. *"But in the days of the voice of the seventh angel, when he shall begin to sound, the mystery of God shall be finished, as he hath declared to his servants the prophets"* (Revelation 10:7).

Chapter 5

Uprising of the Nation of Israelites

The Lord promised to set the Israelites above all other nations on Earth. Regardless to how unfair things may seem today, things in the past were exactly as they should have been when it came to the Israelites having equal rights in the strange land of America. Would you expect to have the same rights visiting your neighbor's house as you would have in your own home? I think not. You can't be a guest in my home and have the same rights and privileges to everything in it as I would. The truth of the matter is that you would have to live with me in my house long enough to earn those rights and privileges. With that being said, now, those rights and privileges have been earned by the Israelites in this country.

The Lord used the Edomites for four centuries punishing and afflicting the Israelites for their disobedience committed in their homeland. However, the time for the afflicting of God's people, the Israelites, in a strange land have come to a close. In the fulfilling of their calling, the Edomites have obeyed God and done their job well. The Israelites have paid the price. All Israelites living in the United States of America can rightfully say, "This is my house now!" We have served our sentence and earned the rights to receive all privileges owed to us.

The writing is on the wall. Israelites and Edomites are now living in the Spiritual Egypt and the Lord is saying, "LET MY PEOPLE GO!" The Father loves His children and is not going back on His word. Prophecy has been fulfilled. The green light was switched on in the eight month of the year 1619. Four centuries have passed. Now the Lord has placed His stop sign at the intersection of the year 2019.

Change is now coming. Dismantling of White supremacy is happening all across the globe. Confederate monuments are being removed worldwide by the same people who placed them there, the Edomites. The children and grandchildren of those which once fought against the Israelites are now fighting for the Israelites. Young nine- and ten-year-old children of all races, are marching with their parents in the streets for change. With the help of cell phones and other technologies, things that had been hidden in the past are now coming to the light. The latest generations are using social media to organize groups against evil forces and create change. The up-and-coming millennials are taking over the powers that be. An evil society is now being exposed. New laws in equality are now being established.

    Prophecy is unfolding right on time. Again, the Lord is saying, "LET MY PEOPLE GO!" Certain people still don't want to be held accountable for their actions and the actions of their ancestors. Yet, they are still benefiting from our years of enslavement. Like the old saying goes, "God works in mysterious ways." Remember when God had to send ten plagues in order to make that happen? According to scripture, in the last plague, God had the Israelites mark their households with blood. His wrath passed over their homes. However, He took the lives of the other homes' firstborn.

The real issues are spiritual. Things are going to turn out exactly as God planned it. It's all about timing and prophecy. For hundreds of years, people have marched and fought against each other for their rights and freedom. However, due to timing and prophecy, all the fighting and marching never really made much of a difference, until now. The fight was never ours to win, and the Lord has already won the fight. *"For we wrestle not against flesh and blood, but against principalities against powers against the rulers of the darkness of this world, against Spiritual wickedness in high places."* (Ephesians 6:12).

Forced to Change

A new plague is now spreading throughout the world. For God's purposes, whatever it may be, the COVID-19 pandemic is spreading throughout the land. The Lord is fighting on behalf of the Israelites. Some can see it, but everyone can't read between the lines. God is using the pandemic to set the stage for His agenda to be heard worldwide. As COVID-19 takes away the lives of people of all races worldwide, suddenly, people around the globe are learning how to come together and stand for a cause worth fighting for.

God decided to sacrifice one of his chosen people from the Tribe of Judah, George Floyd. With people sitting at home with nothing to do and not able to go out and earn money to feed their families, the world witnesses an American Edomite police officer savagely killing an unarmed and handcuffed Israelite on national television with a smirk on his face, and a hand in his pocket. The world pays attention. America has been exposed. Other nations can now see that something had to be done to stop the senseless brutal killings of Israelites in the USA by White police officers.

The timing could not have been more perfect. If the Lord had not sent the global pandemic when He did, the world would not have paid attention to the murder of George Floyd. The people would have been so distracted by making money, sports, and entertainment, nothing else would have mattered. There would have never been a march for civil rights and freedom of all human beings. Neither would the protest for police reform nationwide be taking place. Only God could have put the entire world's focus on this horrific situation.

In the normal state of things, material gain is the primary focus and agenda of people in general. The status quo has changed and things are far from normal. In oppose to all the screaming and hand clapping in the anticipation of who is winning a particular sporting event, people are being forced to focus on things of importance. Like for instance, staying healthy and keeping the entire family healthy. For the sake of their children, parents are now taking a serious look at the situation that the world is in. People are beginning to realize that if they don't fight for changes, their children and grandchildren will inevitably go through the same experiences they had to endure. Society is not used to being put in desperate situations, having to think everything through, and come out safely on the other side.

In the year 2020, COVID-19 has changed the way society functions as a whole. Coronavirus cases are rising steadily all over the world. Many states and countries had to shut down. Wearing a mask in public places has become mandatory in many cities around the world. Due to growing health concerns, social distancing—staying six feet away from everyone in public settings—is a requirement. Temperature checks are mandatory upon entering some public buildings. The number of people attending social gatherings are limited to a bare minimum. Counters are standing outside at the entrance and exit doors, keeping track of the number of people shopping at stores.

People are fearful of visiting their relatives due to the spread of the virus. The disease is so contagious that if a family member gets sick from the virus and have to be hospitalized, you aren't allowed to visit them. With many country borders being closed, people vacationing outside their homeland can't get back to their families. Church services are being held outside of the church buildings in order to slow the spread of the disease. Sporting events which are normally used as a way to get away from all the hustle and bustle of everyday life halted. People are now going stir-crazy, because all major sporting events have been cancelled.

Teaching institutions have gone from teaching in the classrooms to home computer virtual learning. Students graduating in 2020 can no longer experience a traditional graduation ceremony. With bars and nightclubs no longer open, people especially the young are missing out on the nightlife with friends and family. With barber shops, beauty salons, nail shops and gyms closed for months at a time, men and women are walking around looking under the weather. However, the spirit is resilient and we move on.

Propaganda versus Police Reform

Society is beginning to realize that police reform is an aging political propaganda. They have been talking about reform for over fifty years. Through propagandist-controlled mass media, the biased and misleading information of police reform is being promoted and publicized across the country. Broken from the beginning, their official way of policing is unlikely to change when it comes to detaining Israelites across America. Their standard operating procedures has been in place for over four hundred years and has worked very well for the Edomites.

For the purpose of manipulating society into thinking that the Israelites will no longer be shot dead in the streets by White officers, one of the propagandist campaign's new persuasion tactics to placate protestors is painting the words BLACK LIVES MATTER on the streets, highways, and byways in cities across America. The bigger the words painted on the streets, the more likely the propaganda will be believed. We cannot paint racism away. Street renaming and pretty painting does not solve the problems.

This particular propaganda tactic reminds me of how after the assassination of Black activist, Reverend Dr. Martin Luther King Jr. (after they killed him), the Edomites started renaming streets in Dr. King's honor all across America, only to continue killing the Israelites on the very streets renamed in his honor. Street naming and street paintings are nice gestures, however, educating and attacking racism in all American institutions is the one and only solution to the problems of inequity and inequality that plague this country. How effective can police reform be in the United States toward Blacks and Latinos when racism is already engraved in the fabric of society?

The Taking Down of Confederate Monuments

As opposed to fixing the age-old problems in this country, we are seen dancing around them. Even though the Confederate monuments should have never been placed in the prominent places across America to glorify White supremacy and racism, the vandalizing and taking down of the Confederate flags and monuments in the United States does nothing more than add fuel to the flames of racism. It's just a distraction from Satan veering away from the real problems. Oh, you don't like what you see in a Confederate monument... Remember, it's not what you see. It's how you see it.

Well, look at it this way: the same faces you see on these Confederate monuments are the same faces featured on US currency and coins. For instance, President Andrew Jackson owned over a hundred Black men, women, and children slaves. Jackson's photo is prominently featured on the twenty-dollar bill in your wallet. What good would it do for you to burn every twenty-dollar bill you have in your possession? Exactly! The same outcome applies to removing the monuments. Today, over one hundred ten confederate monuments, symbols, and four flags have been removed. The monuments are gone, but the problems and stigma remain.

Two wrongs don't make a right. We would be appalled if they started tearing down what few Black monuments we have. As opposed to desecrating the Confederate monuments from our past, we should be erecting monuments to our modern-day heroes like Angela Davis, Barack Obama, Andrew Young, Reverend Al Sharpton, Reverend Jesse Jackson, and Patrisse

Cullors, to name a few, or we could honor those who have passed away like Rosa Parks, Harriet Tubman, Frederick Douglass, Ronald McNair, and Julian Bond. The list goes on and on.

If we put a statue of Barack Obama next to a monument of Robert E. Lee, it would be a teachable situation. We would be recognizing our past and honoring our present at the same time. Edomites should be ashamed of the history of slavery in this country, but it happened… I can see why they are dragging down Confederate monuments. We shouldn't try to erase the past. We can't change what has already transpired, but we can embrace and learn from the present to build a better future.

Systemic Racism and Racial Disparities

When it comes to building a better future, unity is today's message. However, it is highly unlikely that all nations in the world will do the right thing, which is uniting as one in the fight to stop the spread of COVID-19. Despite all of the "we are united as one" television advertisements seen throughout the world, "United we stand" is only a fallacious perception of reality, regardless to how we perceive it. The reality is that we have a tendency to ignore others when they are in need. The poor will always be with us and so will the rich. Unity among the two classes is extremely unlikely to occur.

We all know that as people we all need the same things. Yet, when it comes right down to it, diversity runs deep. We all bleed red, but the reality is the United States will ignore the needs of the people in China. Just like the people in China will ignore the needs of the people in Africa, and so on. We look out for our own people. Self-preservation is the way of life. That's reality. Divided we stand is a more accurate description of reality. United we stand is only a farfetched perception of reality. However, with that being said, unity is the only way we can build a better tomorrow.

As a nation of people what have we learned from the past? We have learned that what we do today has a direct impact on what takes place tomorrow. When oppression against the Israelites has gone by, we would have learned from the past.

When racial inequality has elapsed in time, we would have learned respect. When we are on the other side of social injustice, we would have learned unity. When acts of violence against the Israelites are bygones, we would have learned justice. Unfortunately, when it comes to these principles, as a country, we are still operating below kindergarten level. We still have much to do and equally much to learn. Until we learn unity and compassion, we can't graduate. Kindergartner's curriculum teaches our five-year-old children simple social skills, such as learning how to play fair, to share, and to respect other people's property and space.

Were the founders of this country taught principles and standards of behavior? Maybe they weren't taught social skills such as how to be a good friend. I remember one of the first things we learned at home, before kindergarten, was to treat others as you would like to be treated. Let's cut to the chase. Actually, there is no excuse for the poor treatment of the Israelites in America because knowing right from wrong is implanted in our hearts.

Kindergartners are old enough to know right from wrong. Through their natural superior logic and reasoning, they don't see the color of skin as a reason to impose violence upon their peers. They only recognize kindness and pain. They embrace being treated with kindness, and they also know when they are being mistreated. To know when you are being mistreated is to know right from wrong.

Regrettably, our Founding Fathers didn't see us as human. Kindergarten curriculum was swept under the rug by our nation's founders. The Israelites sharing the same social territory as the Edomites is still being prevented and shunned by White American citizens to this day.

Black Male Leadership

In order to rise above all nations, as leaders of the Nation of Israelites, we must stand tall and become men. First and foremost, we must respect the order of priorities. With each breath we take, we should remember to put the Lord first in all that we do. *"But I would have you know, that the head of every man is Christ; and the head of every woman is the man; and the head of Christ is God,"* (1 Corinthians 11:3). Israelite males in America have to take back their role as leaders because the hierarchy established by the Father, placed the man in the position of family leadership. The man has to love and respect himself, so he can love and respect his family.

The man has to teach his family Black history which is the Bible. That's the only way his family will know who they are and where they came from. Blacks are not taught Black history in White public schools because Bibles are prohibited in schools. It's the job of Israelite males to teach their children that Jesus was a Black Jew Israelite. This teaching is prohibited in White teaching institutions. Read the Bible and interpret it for yourself. Teach your children the truth. That's how a man begins to show loyalty to God the Father.

The uprising begins when family becomes the priority of the man. It's a man's world. You must be able to lead and fit in at the Round Table. Yet, on the other hand, the woman has to respect the man's role as the head of the household, leading and teaching his family as God has commanded him to do so. The man must look out for his wife and respect their marriage. He should treat his wife like a queen. In return, she must honor him as the king of the castle. We must practice unity. Parents, tell your children that you love them, often. Families be sure to acknowledge each other's accomplishments by lifting each other up.

The father has to teach his children to treat teaching institutions or school as if it were their job. Israelite children must be taught to work twice as hard as their classmates in school. Parents must constantly encourage their children to take in as much knowledge as possible. As we have learned, "Knowledge is power." They must know that they have to become the frontrunners and lead the pack of achievers. Parents, allow your children to get their college degrees while living at home. Teach them to value getting a trade or degree, over moving out into an apartment or home without the tools needed for life.

It's the responsibility of the Israelite men to reteach the Israelite women to respect her nation of Black men. Our impoverished Black Israelite women must look to the Edomites to supply their basic needs of food, health insurance, and housing. The system is purposely set up that way by Edomite men to separate the Israelite men from their family's leadership role. The primary goal is to make Israelite men seem useless to their women and children.

As it were in the days when Blacks were enslaved together on the plantations, being emancipated has never set well with the Edomite nation. I call it "freedom backlash." For example, housing, health care, and food stamps are set up so that the man can't legally live with his woman receiving assistance. If the man is caught living with her, they can both legally be put out to live on the streets. Even though the Black males are underpaid, if they are lucky enough to be gainfully employed at all. The woman, too, often finds herself raising her children without a male role model or physical assistance in the home. She is forced to become the mother and father—a role unfillable by anyone. Especially, young boys need male mentors to aid them in shaping their futures.

While young girls need positive representations of how she should be viewed and treated in this world.

For women, it is a daunting task, but there are some things you can do if you find yourself being a single parent. First, let Christ be your foundation. *"Every good gift and every perfect gift, is from above and cometh down from the Father of lights with whom is no variableness, neither shadow of turning"* (James 1:17). Read the Bible for yourself. Then, get involved in a Christian Church. Make a habit of your children attending, even when you can't. This will give them a sense of hope and self-worth.

Next, lean on your family and friends, male and female, for moral support. Teach and show your children unconditional love. Let them know that who they are as human beings is more important than what they decide to become. Look to their pastor, teachers, and coaches to help you raise them up in the way they ought to go and the Word teaches they won't stray far from it.

Blacks and Browns need to build relationships with banks and bankers. Walk in and introduce yourself. Let them know who you are as apart of the community. Talk with them about their and your families. Brag on your children and listen to the banker's interest. Let them know you support local businesses, and when you go in to do your banking, greet them by name. Let them know you see them as an ally, and if you ever need a loan or their assistance, you will come to them personally.

Israelites need to frequent Black- and Brown-owned businesses as often as possible. Money talks... We have to support each other. Where we spend our dollars determines who survives and who goes under. We've been conditioned to think our businesses can't give or don't provide quality customer service. Nothing could be further from the truth. It goes back to Jim Crow laws designed to separate and cause chaos in Black communities. Small and minority-owned businesses take pride and personal responsibility in their services.

Set an example for your offspring. Be independent and teach independence to your children. Give or let them earn their allowance. Teach them the importance of saving their allowance in a piggy bank. Be sure that they know how much money they have before they decide how much of their money they can spend. As they start growing into young adults, step the training up a notch. Teach them the importance of being smart with the spending of their money. We are to teach our children to spend their own money—not others—and to live within, not above, their financial means. Children need to know that borrowing other people's money will cost them a lot more money in the long run.

Familiarize them with how credit cards work. They need to know that credit cards authorize them to purchase things that they don't have the immediate money to pay for. Why keep borrowing month after month, when you can be saving month after month? Let them know that the lenders have made their own set of rules. The rules are, when you use their credit card, you must pay the cost of the purchase and agree to pay extra charges and fees. Make them aware that they should be the lenders, not borrowers. Teach your children that managing their money is one of the certainties in life that they must take full control of. Avoid credit card debt because through default, it can quickly get ahead of their finances as interest and other month-to-month penalties accumulate.

Every child has a dream of some sort. The problem is that most children are not encouraged early enough in life to go after their dreams. The reason they don't go after their dream is because they never developed a sense of purpose in life. It's important that each individual child realize their purpose in life. It is vital because by helping your children realize their purpose, you are helping them realize their dreams. Some parents make the mistake of pushing their own dreams and aspirations upon their children.

For the most part, children naturally follow in the footsteps of their parents anyway. By not knowing or developing their own purpose or realizing their own dreams, many children get caught up in their parents' dream. Like, for instance, running a family business. That's okay, because the parents may one day pass that business on to them, giving them a purpose and a dream. If the family business survives, it could be passed down from generation to generation.

Avoid leaving your children empty-handed. Make a will, buy life insurance, and leave an inheritance. The average White family rises above Black families financially through their inheritance. Black children in the United States generally inherit less money and property than their White counterparts. The fact is, due to many centuries of systematic racism and wage inequality for the people who have had to work a nine-to-five job for a living, Blacks in the US have always been paid less than Whites on every educational level.

Therefore, over the course of many centuries, White families, being paid more money, were able to accumulate great wealth and pass it down to their children. When wage inequality no longer exists in this country, more Black Israelites will be able to inherit great wealth to be passed down to their children over the centuries. Then, they will be able to invest and erect more structures and skyscrapers throughout this country.

After you succeed, you should want to pay it forward. There is nothing wrong with reaching back and helping another Israelite succeed. Even if you move out or on from your community, you may want to get involved with your old community by making yourself, as well as your resources, available. At the end of the day, it shouldn't always be about monetary gain. Your selflessness of making a contribution to your community that you were raised up in goes a long way. It will also bring pride, honor, and prestige to you as the contributor.

Being in the spotlight of your success, people will want to imitate you. This also gives you an opportunity to mentor and be a role model to other people in your old community, especially the younger group. By doing so, your success will be emulated by other Israelites in your community. Having you as a mentor, others will match and surpass your success.

Israelites must keep up with current events. We know that global current events have always been of political and social importance worldwide. Today's news briefs, often concerning critical government decisions, medical discoveries, and technology breakthroughs will have a direct and immediate effect on your life. The way things are going today, current world leaders should be everyone's concern. Therefore, by keeping up with current events, you will know about new laws and legislation that effect your life. Civil rights activists, like the late John Lewis, one of the original thirteen Freedom Riders, and many others went to jail, fought, and were willing to die for us to have the right to vote. As parents, it's your responsibility to teach your children to vote and get involved with local and national politics.

Reading should also be a top priority of all people. You can easily travel the world in a book. By taking a little time out of a day to read, your knowledge as well as your communication skills will improve. Reading offers us a goldmine of learning and makes us smarter. Your children should take pride in saying the following statements: "As for me, I love reading. So if you want to hide something from me, you better not put it in a book, because I'm going to find it."

Stop Black-on-Black crime. During protests, stop raiding and looting Black neighborhoods and businesses. They are not the problem. We should be able to peacefully gather to make our voices and demands heard. When you see injustices, stand up and protest or take it up on social media. Whether it's Black-on-Black or police-on-Black, we can no longer sit idly by while Israelites are being mowed down in the streets.

Don't give the police a reason to target you. As if they need one. Keep your vehicle up to code. Don't drink and drive, and don't speed. Learn to resolve domestic disputes with words, not violence. Obey the laws of God, as well as the laws of the land. Do what you can to handle arguments within your own home. Happening for hundreds of years now, time and time again, in many cases, Black women call on Edomite police officers to help settle a family dispute between her and the husband, or sometimes other family members. As opposed to the dispute being settled by the officers, either the husband, wife, or family member ends up in jail or even worse, being shot to death by White police officers. We really don't need that any more.

The fewer calls we make to the police, the less they will be in our communities to harass and be in our business. We must learn to rely on our clergy and trusted family members to referee. If we can form gangs, we can get teens involved in community watch, sports, and boys' and girls' clubs. Join organizations like Big Brother and Big Sister of America and help mentor our youth. Today's youth are not waiting on the older generation to fix the problems that they will have to face in the future. The new generation of youth have learned new ways of getting involved and being active in today's social advocacy. As they look back at the last fifty years and look forward toward their own future, they can no longer ignore the desperate need for social change, and they are doing what it takes to make those changes happen.

Chapter 6

Consequences for Disobedience

God is a spirit of everlasting calmness. As Lord of the universe, He punishes and eradicates sin in order to keep His Spirit free from agitation, disturbance, and any form of violent activity. Quite the opposite from human beings. As sinful nations of people, we are agitated spirits of rebellion, unruliness, often showing strong emotions. In the effort to make us become more like Him, for our own good, God has to soften and restrain our disorderly spirit so that we may reflect His own image. The spirit has a way of wanting to establish its own will and do things its own way, pushing God's will aside. Since the destiny of the spirit is under God's control, there's nothing we can do to change the events that are necessary for the taming of our spirit.

To remedy the problem of defiance, people not being willing to do what the Lord has commanded us to do: Putting us in captivity would be the best way to go about suppressing and conquering our spirit. It's the best method of breaking an evil spirit. As harsh as it may seem, a lifetime of captivity is the most effective way to soften, and eventually subdue our spirit into obedience. God never really wanted anyone to live their whole life in captivity. However, knowing what would be best for us, He just wanted us to obey Him. In hindsight, which is 20/20, we as a people should have been in compliance to God's every word from the beginning. He is a more merciful leader than the people who took us captive.

The Lord had to change the status quo of plan A to plan B. The renewal of the status quo to plan B exchanged freedom for bondage and violent activity. Israelites being persecuted and forced to wander in the Egyptian wilderness from place to place looking for food, water, and shelter was punishment for their disobedience. Being confined and enslaved by the Egyptians has now broken the unity and completeness of our spirit with God the Father. Feeling as though we have to fin for ourselves, a metamorphosis has occurred in the spirit of the Israelites.

The Captivities

The Lord purposed the first forced detention of the Jews to take place in Egypt. Under the leadership of Pharaoh, the Egyptians imprisoned and confined the Israelite men and women to heavy slave labor. He had them working outside in the elements from sunup to sundown. They were supervised by harsh taskmasters, who were purposely making each task more difficult for the enslaved Jews to keep up with the expected daily work quota. The heat from the sun bore down on the sweaty backs of the slaves as they served their masters for food, water, and shelter. They felt as though they were all alone, having no one to rescue them from prolonged cruel and unjust treatment. These harsh conditions would cause the Israelites to reminisce about the years when they were free.

When, on the other hand, the Lord was working in their favor to free them from their captors. Being the spokesman for God, the Prophet Moses told Pharaoh that God commanded him to let His people go in order that they may serve Him. Pharaoh, looking at the objective outcome of freeing the slaves, became very agitated and disturbed. The expectation of losing his free laborers did not sit well with him. For that reason, God had to send ten plagues upon the land of Egypt before Pharaoh came to his senses and freed the Israelites.

Witnessing the freedom walk of the slaves grieved Pharaoh's heart in such a way that he changed his mind and aspired to recapture God's people and bring them back into bondage. With regard to the king wanting to recapture them, Pharaoh never actually let the people go, so the Egyptians unsuccessfully chased after the Israelites. Finally, Pharaoh saw the Children of Israel in the midst of the sea, walking on dry land, moving out of the Egyptian captivity. In the end, the Lord shows Pharaoh and the rest of the world how He felt about the captivity of the Israelites by drowning the king's army in the Red Sea.

As time went on, Nebuchadnezzar had become the king of Babylon. The Lord protected and never gave up on his people. Nonetheless, due to the arrogance of the Israelites, they were still being disobedient to God in their own land. This provoked God to anger. Captivity again would be the Lord's choice of education and punishment. God would have to subdue the rebellious spirits of the Israelites by taking them into a second captivity. Living in captivity for seventy years would soon become the way of life for the Israelites.

The next forced detention of the Israelites would be the Babylonian captivity which paved the way to the fall of Jerusalem. According to 2 Kings chapter 24, with God being in control, He sent their enemies against them. The Babylonian army attacked and captured the Israelites. During the attack, by force, the army took over ten thousand Israelite men captive from their homeland of Jerusalem. The Lord had the Babylonian army carry the Israelites off into Babylon for seventy years of grueling captivity.

Not only that, to further vanquish their spirits, the army destroyed most of Jerusalem. They burned down the temple and stole all of the gold and treasures of King Solomon's house. Only the weak were left behind to live in Jerusalem. At the end of the seventy years, the Babylonian captivity ended in the first year of the reign of Cyrus, the king of Persia. Cyrus sent the Israelites back to Jerusalem for God's purpose. Later, the Lord instructed King Cyrus to decree that the temple in Jerusalem be reconstructed for the Children of Israel, which they did.

The Lord has proclaimed that those that lead people into captivity will one day also be taken into captivity. "What's good for the monkey is also good for the gorilla." As a turn of events, the Persian Captivity happened when the Babylonians were forced into exile by Medes and the Persians while King Cyrus still ruled bringing the Babylonian empire to an end. At last, they remembered their harsh treatment toward the Israelites. Ironically, the Babylonians, once the capturers, became the captive.

Jerusalem, the city of God (the homeland of the Black Jew Israelites) was seized and conquered in 63 BCE under the Edomite General Pompey. It marked the beginning of the Roman Captivity. In the settlement of the 63 BCE Roman Captivity, Jerusalem became a satellite city of the Roman Republic. Jerusalem, the capital of the state of Israel became economically, politically, and militarily dependent on Rome, and still is to this day.

The Roman captivity will be stretched out until Jesus returns. It seems to me as though the White man wants to unjustly rule the world. Yet the world will eventually be ruled with the Lord's rod of justice. Wanting to be God, the Edomites (White man) feel entitled to take God's land from His children, the Israelites. You see, Jerusalem belongs to God, and no one will ever have the power to take it from Him. Being the capital of Israel and one of the oldest cities in the world, Jerusalem is the city God chose for the Children of Israel. *"But I have chosen Jerusalem, that my name might be there: and have chosen David to be over my people Israel"* (2 Chronicles 6:6).

The Edomites feel like this: Since we can't capture or put God into captivity, let's do it to his children and take their land from them. They would say things like! "How is your God going to stop us from seizing Jerusalem?" "Who owns the land now?" "Where is your God?" They didn't realize that the Lord was right there listening and laughing at their foolish comments. The Lord's prophecy will prevail.

However long it may take, the Roman captivity of Jerusalem will end when Christ returns to reign forever from the Holy Land as the King of the Jews. Justice will prevail and the Lord will return the land back to The Children of Israel, forever. *"And I John saw the holy city, New Jerusalem, coming down from God out of heaven, prepared as a bride adorned for her husband. And I heard a great voice out of Heaven saying, Behold, the tabernacle of God is with men, and he will dwell with them, and they shall be his people, and God himself shall be with them, and be their God"* (Revelation 21:2–3) The Roman Captivity of Jerusalem has ended and the Edomite capturers will be taken into captivity and held captive in Hell, forever.

Abraham Fathers the Israelite Nation

All of the nations of people that live on the Earth today, came out of the loins of Noah and his three sons, Shem, Ham, and Japheth. The world's growing population of seven point eight billion (7,800,000,000) people extends from the eight people that came out of the Ark after the great flood that lasted forty days and forty nights. Furthermore, according to the Bible, Noah descended from Adam, who is the father of the human race. Created from dirt, Adam and Eve were formed. The same type of dirt that we use to grow our crops is the same type that God used to form the bodies of Adam and Eve. In the beginning, the population of the Earth came from the seed of Adam, reflecting the color of dirt as well as the image of God.

Your nationality, whatever it may be, comes from the seed of your father. The body of your mother is like the soil that grows the seed. It's not always about color. For instance, if the father is Black and the mother is White, or vice versa, the true nationality of the child will come from the seed of the Father. Take for example, you can take an apple seed and plant it anywhere on Earth in various types of soil, you'll notice that regardless to what type of soil the seed was planted in, it can only grow and produce the apple tree which comes from the seed itself.

The first nation of people emerged through natural order. From the seeds of the Israelites, the founding fathers of the human race, came all other nations of people here on Earth. Three Black men; Shem, Ham, and Japheth, the sons of Noah, along with their wives started the repopulation of the human race extending across the globe. *"And God spoke unto Noah, and to his sons with him, saying. And I, behold, I establish my covenant with you, and with your seed after you"* (Genesis 9:8–9). The seed God is speaking of here in the scripture is Abraham, Isaac, Jacob, and the Children of Israel. Years later, coming from the bloodline of the Tribe of Judah, came the Black

Jew, Jesus Christ, The Son of God to reestablish the Covenant of the Father.

Lot Fathers the Japanese and Chinese Nations

The second and third nation of people on Earth according to Genesis chapter 19, would be the Moabite (Asian-Chinese) and Ammonite (Japanese) Nation of people. A man named Lot, is the father of the Japanese and Chinese nations of people worldwide. Before the destruction of Sodom and Gomorrah, the Lord sent two angels to tell Lot to take his family and leave the city. Lot greeted the angels by bowing down with his head toward the ground. Just so you know, from the mannerism of the man Lot in the Bible came the Japanese and Chinese social etiquette of greeting a person by bowing, as opposed to a handshake.

Here is how the two nations came to be. Lot took the advice of the two angels. He took his wife and his two daughters and left the city. The Lord had warned them to leave the city and not look back. As the Lord rained fire and brimstone from the sky upon the city, Lot, his wife and their two daughters were running away. However, as they were running Lot's wife decided to look back at the burning city. When she turned and looked back, she instantly turned into a pillar of salt. Eventually, Lot and his two daughters went up into the mountains and dwelt in a cave.

Fearing they would be the last people alive on Earth, the oldest daughter suggested to her younger sister, saying, "Daddy is an old man, and we don't have anyone else to have sex with us and get us pregnant. Let's get Daddy drunk with some wine, have sex with him, and have his child in order that we can preserve the seed of our father." They agreed to it. That same night they got their father so drunk that he did not know what happened. The oldest daughter laid with him and got pregnant that night.

When the next day came around, the younger sister told the oldest sister, "Let's get Daddy drunk again and tonight, I will lay with him and get pregnant and preserve the seed of our father." So they got their father drunk that night. The youngest sister laid with him and got pregnant. Now both of the daughters were pregnant with a child by their father. *"And the firstborn bare a son, and called his name Moab: the same is the father of the Moabites unto this day. And the younger, she also bare a son, and called his name Benammi: the same is the father of Ammon unto this day"* (Genesis 19:37–38).

Esau Fathers the Edomite Nation

Abraham, Isaac, and Jacob are the three Patriarchs of the Israelite nation. However, Isaac and Rebekah were the parents of the last nationality of people procreated known as the Edomites, White people. During the course of Rebekah's pregnancy, she noticed that the children seemed to be fighting in her womb. She went to the Lord in prayer and asked Him why the children were struggling inside her. The Lord told the Israelite Rebekah that two nations were in her womb. He also said that one shall be stronger than the other and one shall serve the other.

The first came out red all over like a hairy garment and they called his name Esau. After that came his brother with his hand holding Esau's heel; and they named him Jacob. Esau, the cunning hunter grew up in the mountains of Seir, married his wife Adah, and became the father of the Edomite nation of White people. *Thus dwelt Esau in mount Seir: Esau is Edom. And these are the generations of Esau the father of the Edomites in mount Sier"* (Genesis 36:8–9).

Esau, the father of the Edomites, moved his inheritance from Canaan and established his living quarters high up in the mountains of Mount Sier. He inherited so much livestock that he had to find a new territory to support his family and his wealth. It's by nature that the Edomite nation of White people has always wanted to sit high and look low just like their father, Esau. Being the cunning hunters, by sitting high and looking low, they are in a better position to see and control their prey. In a social setting, the elevation puts the Edomites in a better financial position to do as they please.

By sitting in high political offices, and feeling superior, the Edomites have created a system of wage disparity among them and the Israelites in the United States in order that they may look down upon them as an inferior nation of people. Yet the Lord has already established the Children of Israel (Jacob) above all other nations on Earth. However, the Edomites have always hated and believed they are superior to the Israelites. The fact is, White people have the blood of Esau flowing through their veins. They hate us, but we can't afford to hate them. Only God has the right to hate anyone. God reminded us of this. *"I have loved you saith the Lord. Yet ye say. Wherein hast thou loved us? Was not Esau Jacob's brother? Saith the Lord: yet I have loved Jacob. And I hated Esau, and laid his mountains and his heritage waste for the dragons of the wilderness"* (Malachi 1:2–3).

The Lord has good reasons for hating Esau and his inheritance. The social norms of theft and murdering Israelites in the United States has been passed down from Esau's heritage. The truth is, Esau's posterity continues today. It's been passed down from generation to generation and has become the Western Civilization. Esau's heritage was first passed down from Edom, to the Roman Empire. The Roman Empire had the audacity to put Jerusalem (*The City of God*) in captivity making it economically and politically dependent on Rome. How could something like that sit well with God?

Furthermore, the heritage of Esau continued from Rome to modern Europe and passed on to the United States. The Edomites pillaged the land from the ten tribes of Israel the Native Americans and claimed it as their own. The Edomites took over by hunting them down and killing them with their superior weapons and natural instincts. America was founded on the bloodshed of the Israelites. *"So ye shall not pollute the land wherein ye are: for blood defiles the land: and the land cannot be cleansed of the blood that is shed therein, but by the blood of him that shed it"* (Numbers 33:35). Still, in today's modern society here in the United States, God's chosen nation of people the Israelites are looked down upon by the White Edomites. What more could they want from the Israelites? The blood of their precious children is the only thing left to be taken from them.

The Ultimate Sacrifice

The blood that flows through everyone's veins giving all of us life is our gift from God. Blood is holy and has a holy voice. To get a better understanding of blood and how it effects the land we live on, we have to go back to the beginning where the first recorded murder was committed. When Cain killed his brother Abel, the Lord spoke to him and said, "The voice of thy brother's blood cry's out to me from the ground. The mouth of the ground has opened up and received your brother's blood." Nothing has changed. Till this day, when a murder is committed, the blood cry's out to the Lord when the body passes away. You see, our blood demands justice from God!

As the Edomites were slaughtering the Native Americans (Natives of Arsareth), the voices in the Holy Blood that fell on the ground cried out to God for justice. By murdering the Israelites, the homeland was being defiled by the Edomites. By taking the land, the Edomites were able to establish their own laws which enabled them to avoid arrest and persecution. As fugitives, they spend their whole lives running and hiding from God to avoid punishment. All of the people that have murdered the Natives of Arsareth/America remain fugitives to God's justice. Even if they had been charged with their crimes of murder, and served jail time here on Earth (which they did not), they would still remain fugitives to the Lord's justice their entire life.

According to scripture, murderers are fugitives that will live unsettled lives awaiting God's justice. Meaning, no one ever gets away with murder, regardless of how things may appear on Earth. Because of the Lord's holiness, sin has to be punished and justice must be served as well. Only God has the right to spill a person's blood and take their life from them. Remember when the Lord said vengeance is mine.

Blood has a deep connection with the spirit of God. The same blood that flowed in the veins of Jesus Christ while He lived on the Earth is the same blood that flows in the veins of the Israelites today. Related by blood and sharing ancestors the Israelites are the blood relatives of the Son of God. Everything involving our kinship with God the Father is encased in the blood of His Son. It's the blood of Jesus Christ that proclaimed the utmost offering to His Father.

With God, blood is personal. His blood and His life is all about holiness. Because the Lord is holy, He needs us to be holy as well. Being His children, we have His blood, but we have an obedience problem. Sin is the one thing that cannot coexist with God. God is a sin killer. Because God the Father is a merciful God and loves His children, He had to establish creative ways of killing sin without killing us. That's when He decided to use objects of atonement that bleed, such as goats, sheep, and birds that we could offer Him for our sins. Animal blood would be the payment required by God for the debt of sin.

As for Adam and Eve disobeying the Lord's command, the first sin was touching and eating the fruit of the tree in the midst of the Garden of Eden. Being the merciful God that He is, out of love, to avoid killing Adam and Eve, the first animal blood sacrifice had to take place. He loved us so much that He didn't want to leave Adam and Eve naked and afraid in the woods. So prior to sending them away from the garden, He had to kill and sacrifice the blood of an animal for their sin. Because God doesn't do anything for just one reason, at the same time the Lord decided to make Adam and Eve (clothing) coats of skins to cover their nakedness.

These coats of animal skin clothing had power, and were durable enough to last over a thousand years. Second Samuel 1:18 references the Book of Jasher, which records the passing down of these garments that God had made. They were first passed down from Adam to Methuselah. Now Methuselah lived 969 years and passed the garments down to Noah. Noah took the garments with him on the Ark. Eventually, these holy garments were passed down to Noah's grandson Nimrod, which ruled with the same coats of skins that were made from the first blood sacrifice recorded in the Bible. No one knows what happened to the garments after Esau murdered King Nimrod and stole them.

To reiterate, blood is sacred to God. All throughout the Old Testament in the Bible, in order to keep from killing us for our disobedience, the bloody sacrifices of sheep, birds, and goats were required as an offering to the Lord for the payments of our sins. From the Father in Heaven, His merciful Son Jesus Christ was given permission to come down from Heaven and rescue us from our sins. His feelings for us goes far beyond friendship. Jesus knowing that He would have to pay with His blood was sacrificed, paying for our debt of sins and giving us the right to be with Him and His Father in Heaven. The blood of Jesus Christ is the ultimate sacrifice.

Almighty God versus the Almighty Dollar

Jesus Christ loves us so much that He has paid off our debts of sin with His blood. In an exchange for His payment, most of today's society completely ignores the word of the Almighty God, and praises the almighty dollar in His place.

Humanity has crossed over the line. Currency is the god that most people are praising. People serve whomever or whatever they love. Never being satisfied, the accumulation of wealth is the common agenda among most people. Even if it means compromising spiritual morality, people will do whatever it takes to gain wealth. Only a few among us are content with what we have been blessed with.

Being total opposites, there is a wide space between greed and contentment, and even a wider space between the Almighty God and the almighty dollar. The Lord is wise and already knows what our needs are. We, on the other hand, think we know what our needs are. Even though it's better to have and not need than to need and not have, the Lord uses His wisdom to bless us in His time. So not being content with what God has already blessed us with is not appreciating God's wisdom.

Being egotistical creatures, we must learn that it's not about what we want and when we want it. Rather, it's about what the Lord wants to bless us with, and when He wants to bless us. God needs people to praise Him for who He is, as opposed to praising currency and wealth for what it is. Greed is one of the seven most deadly sins. It causes nations to praise money and materials things in oppose to praising God Himself. We can look around us and see that praising the Lord and obeying His word is not the priority of most people living in America. For the majority of people in today's society, having a strong desire to possess great wealth is their primary agenda.

In dire need of straightening, our priorities are bent by society. For the most part, many are focused on the short term (temporal) needs of this life, as opposed to being focused on the long term (eternal) needs of the next life. "Birds of a feather flock together." Wealthy people are not seen hanging out with the homeless. The elite, having the most, seem to be loved the most, and those who are poor and have less, seem to be loved less. However, in actuality, usually it's the poor (God-fearing people) that possess the true riches through their relationship with the Lord. *"No one can serve two masters. Either you will hate the one and love the other, or you will be devoted to the one and despise the other, you cannot serve both God and money"* (Luke 16:13).

The primary reason we can't serve God and money is that the Lord is sitting on the throne and currency is one of the modern-day false gods. When your concept of having money has dethroned God, it becomes an idol. The serving of idols angers God. The Lord warned the Israelites numerous times to not turn to idols and serve them. That's why He spoke and said, *"I am the Lord your God."* Yet, here in America, the affections of societies in the Western Civilization are set on praising another master, unworthy of being praised—money.

Everything that the Lord does is praiseworthy. Christ, knowing that His Father's children aren't happy being outside their natural spiritual habitat, has done everything that's necessary for our return to the Father. The highest praise extends out to the one who has paid the cost of sins without disparity for all the nations of people on the Earth. Could you even imagine the type of world we would be living in if God's laws were set up like the laws of the United States Constitution? Nations of people living on the same land would not have the right to breathe the same air as others.

Praiseworthy is the one who supplies the same amount of air, without inequality, for the Israelites to breathe as He does for the Edomites. Being a just God with just laws, He sends the same amount of sunshine without variation upon the Edomites as He does the Israelites. Without discrepancy among certain people, we all share the same rights and privileges of the laws of God: "One nation under God… With liberty and justice for all." The previous quotes, have never applied to people of color here in the United States of America. In other words, the Pledge of Allegiance to the Flag serves Edomites only.

On the other hand, praiseworthy is the one that sends the same amount of rain without imbalance, upon the Israelites as He does the Edomites. Without prejudice, anybody, regardless of race are entitled to build a nurturing relationship with God the Father through His Son, Jesus Christ. The Lord being a just God, doesn't have unjust hatred toward certain nations of people. Everyone has been given a fair chance to the equal rights and privileges of the Father through Christ. Praiseworthiness falls upon the Lord.

The Diminishing of the Israelites Culture

The humble beginnings of the Israelite culture started out with the tilling of their own land and growing crops in their homeland. Disobedience on their part caused the Lord to send their enemies after them which resulted in the Israelites being captured and taken away to a foreign land. Nonetheless, after being kidnapped and enslaved by the Edomites, the Israelites began to adopt the cultural ways of their capturers.

After destroying the culture of the Israelites through slavery, on January 16, 1865, the freed slaves were promised a chance to return to their own culture of tilling the grounds of their own land. Yet, the promise turned out to be a lie. According to a part of Special Field Orders No. 15, the Post-Civil War promise proclaimed by General William Tecumseh was that freed slaves would receive restitution of forty acres of land and a mule. Then they would be able to till their own land and grow their own crops as it were in the beginning of their culture in the land of Canaan.

Happening days after the Edomites promise of forty acres and a mule, the same people that made that promise backed down from it. They fought and died in the Civil War to keep the Israelites enslaved. It turned out that the Edomites of the Confederacy lost the war, and likewise, the Israelites lost their forty acres of land and their mule. Now being freed from slavery with no land and no money in a foreign country, the Israelites were forced to adapt to the Edomites wicked culture of the Western Civilization. The freed nation of Israelites lowered their moral standards. This new American culture would go against their own ways as well as the Laws of God.

The uprooting of the Israelite customs began with the separation of the family members. Being caught up in the midst of slavery, multiple generations of family members of the Israelites had already been separated by slave masters. The inability of the families to be reunited again was the first nail in the coffin for the Israelite ways of life. The continuity of family had always been first and foremost in the culture of the Israelites.

The pillar that solidifies the strength of the Israelites lies within the collectivist culture of their own people. Blacks came in together on ships and went into slavery. After being freed from slavery, we should have reunited as a nation, and came out on top. However, most of us went our own ways. As a destroyed nation of people, we were fearful and hadn't learned how to stand and work collectively together outside the plantations. From years past, there has always been safety in numbers. Yet the Israelite nation, in part due to the Jim Crow Laws, never connected the dots. "United we stand, and divided we fall."

The greatest mistake ever made by the Israelites was not coming back together as a nation. Instead, we joined in with the Edomite's culture in order to fit in. By doing so, we have gone from being a collective group and became one with the American culture of individualism. Losing our original families, being placed into new families and given American names has put us in the middle of the American Edomite melting pot. Being a destroyed nation, the Israelites would do anything to fit in with society. Being ashamed of their hair, the Blacks began perming their natural wooly hair in exchange for the natural straight hair look of White people. Then taking it a step further, being ashamed of their skin tones, they started bleaching their skin to look more like the Edomites.

Being God's chosen nation of people, the Lord spoke with the Israelites warning them to not sleep with, neither marry outside their nation. According to the Scriptures, the Edomites have always been the enemies of the Israelites. However, the practice of interracial marriages has always been a part of the culture of Westerners. It started with the Edomites sleeping with and eventually marrying enslaved Israelite women. After being freed from slavery, some of the Israelites married White Edomites for social status and financial gain.

Many Black women are more attracted to White men than the Blacks because of finances, and the same for Black men. Lucrative incomes lead to a better quality of life here on Earth. However, the Lord spoke to the Israelites saying, *"Keep thee away from the strange woman"* (Proverbs 7:5). The strange woman in the Bible means a woman that is not of your father's seed. Israelite men are not to sleep with or marry strange women. As the father is the head of Christ, the man is the head of the woman. Therefore, the responsibility of teaching Israelite women about their father's seed falls upon the shoulders of Israelite men. It's a difficult task!

Remember when God said, Adam and Eve are one flesh, and He called their name Adam? Eve did what she wanted to do. Today's young women know what's right and what's wrong in God's eyes. The Lord Himself told Eve to not eat of the forbidden tree in the midst of the garden. Yet she ate of it anyway. The outcome would be the same. With both of them knowing right from wrong and eating of the tree, The Bible says that the woman was in transgression, not the man (1 Timothy 2:14). If Eve had not disobeyed God, women's rights in America would still prevail in the present time. People have the right to fall in love with only who God says it's okay to fall in love with. Regardless of how much Israelite men love strange women, their feelings will never trump over God's word.

The man carries the seed and the Lord wants to preserve the purity in the seed of the Israelite nation. Marrying many strange women was the downfall of King Solomon. *"But King Solomon loved many strange women, together with the daughter of Pharaoh, women of the Moabites, Ammonites, Edomites, Zidonians, and Hittites: Of the nations concerning which the Lord said unto the Children of Israel, Ye shall not go in to them, neither shall they come into you; for surely they will turn away your heart after their God: Solomon clave into these in love"* (1 Kings 11:1–2).

When it comes to culture, not much has changed. Back in the day, thousands of years ago, many women from the other nations were attracted to the Israelite King Solomon because of his riches. Other nations of people are allowed to marry into other nations. On the other hand, being an Israelite, knowing that you are set apart by God from the other nations, you are not allowed. So people say. "Excuse me! I fell in love with her for all the right reasons. We know it's against God's word, but He understands!" Really? Jesus said, "If you love me you will keep my commandments." The question is, who do you really love?

For a male Israelite to marry a female not of his father's seed is adapting to the American cultural ways of the Edomite nation. What we must understand is that the Lord has higher purposes for everything He does. The Lord has the right to tell Israelite men not to marry outside His nation of chosen people. It's not His job to cater to us. It's our job to cater to Him. The Israelites are the nation of people that God created on His land and put in charge to lead all other nations and fulfill His purposes. The seeds of Israel are high on God's pedestal.

The Israelites Glorifying the World

The Israelite ways are further diminished through the lure of American entertainment. Having and looking forward to having a lot of fun each day is not being sinful. The Lord wants His children to have fun. However, the idle mind craves mindless entertainment. It's known as the Devil's workshop. As a part of the American culture, mindless entertainment does a lot more than help you get away from the hustle and bustle of life and relaxing the mind. Worldly entertainment is designed by Satan to take your mind off of God.

In the culture of true Israelites, they would spend most of their time glorifying the things of the Lord by worshiping Him daily with lots of zeal. God's chosen people are put in charge to be role models to the rest of the nations. Instead, here in Arsareth/America, some of the Israelites have fallen into the habit of chasing other nation's joys through the many forms of worldly entertainment. For hundreds of years now, the Israelites have been forced into living through a cultural shock here in America. People in general spend their days either glorifying things of God or glorifying things of the world. Life provides us with the choices. Regardless of how you look at it, one is always chosen over the other. The wrong choice has dangerous consequences.

When Israelites spend most of their free time seeking entertainment from the things of the world, as opposed to gravitating toward the things of the Lord, such as prayer and living a godly life, it rightfully provokes the Lord to anger. His children are glorifying idols and false Gods instead of glorying in the true God the Father. It's easy to get caught up in all the screaming, hand clapping, and praising other people. The Israelite nation is spending too much time with their attention and interest focused on movies, TV shows, books, food festivals, amusement parks, professional sports players, and numerous sporting events. This is a culture shock indeed. True Israelites should spend more time glorifying the Lord than anything else.

As a part of the American society, more of us are openly glorifying the players of professional sports while less of us are seen glorifying the Lord. As for the Israelites putting people on a pedestal, remember, the Bible says, "God is a jealous God" (Exodus 20:5). The Father forbids us to put sports and entertainment above Him. The Lord wants and needs to be the only one holding the attention of the nations.

The Judicial System from God to the Israelites

The Lord is the God of Justice. Have you ever wondered how the term judicial system evolved? It originated from the Israelite Tribe of Judah in the Bible. The term originally evolved from the Israelites thousands of years ago. From the Bible, the term *judicial system* stems from the name of the fourth son of Jacob (Israel), Judah. The Lord proclaims that Jacob's son Judah is His lawgiver. This judicial system given to Judah from God was meant to administer justice based on fairness, impartial, and just treatment without favoritism or discrimination. Quite the opposite of today's White man's judicial system of justice.

The judicial powers has departed from the Israelites. God's judicial system that had been given to the Israelites has been stolen and perverted by the Edomites. It's been going on for hundreds of years now. The judicial structure of the White man's justice is based on unfairness, favoritism, and discrimination, especially against the Israelites. In fact, the dispensation of justice here in the United States is unethical. Their organizations and judicial powers administer justice as, whatever, the Edomites decides is fair. Most often not according to uprightness.

Here is what the Lord has to say about the Israelites and the Edomites judicial system. *"Gilead is mine, and Manasseh is mine: Ephraim also is the strength of mine head; Judah is my lawgiver; Moab is my washpot; over Edom will I cast out my shoe: Philistia, triumph thou because of me"* (Psalm 60:7–8). The Black Israelite tribe of Judah, which is the same tribe Jesus Christ sprang forth from, is the lawgiver of God. At some point in time, the judicial system will rightfully be returned back to the Israelites.

Since the Edomites has perverted justice and attempted to dethrone the lawgiver, God will cast out his shoe over the Edomites for the unjust dealings with His Chosen nation of people, the Israelites. Then the enemies of the Israelites shall be destroyed by the Lord as it is written in prophecy. In the end, the judicial system will operate in fairness, with impartial and just treatment without favoritism or any form of discrimination against His children. When the justice of God prevails, the Israelites will have returned to being the lawgivers as they were originally intended in the beginning.

The Evolution of the Medical Logo Came from Israelites

Have you ever wondered where the medical logo came from? Well, it came from the Bible. The serpent coiled around a pole, plastered on medical buildings and on ambulances worldwide, represents the Lord's way of healing the Israelites. It was originally intended to save the lives of the Israelites that were bitten by poisonous snakes in the wilderness. The idea of creating an emblem of a snake coiled around a pole seen worldwide on ambulances and pharmaceutical packaging came from the word of God. The truth behind the emblem is that God commanded Moses to make a bronze snake and set it on a pole to save the lives of the Israelites that were bitten by snakes in the wilderness.

As Moses led the Israelites through the wilderness to go around Edom and the Edomites, the Israelites complained among themselves about the lack of food and water in the wilderness. As they spoke against God and against Moses, it provoked the Lord to anger. So He sent venomous snakes among the complaining Israelites to bite and kill many of them. After many were bitten and had died from snake bites, they confessed to Moses that they had spoken against him and God. They asked him to pray to God that He would take the snakes away from them.

Moses prayed for them. To remedy the problem of the serpents, the Lord commanded Moses to make a bronze snake and put it up on a pole to restore the health of anyone bitten by one of the snakes. From that point on, anyone that was bitten by a poisonous snake could simply look upon the bronze snake that was on the pole and have their health restored and live. *"And the Lord said unto Moses, Make thee a fiery serpent, and set it upon a pole; and it shall come to pass, that every one that is bitten, and he looketh upon it shall live"* (Numbers 21:8).

Now you have the Biblical truth behind the logo seen on medical buildings, pharmaceutical labels, and ambulances throughout the world. To this day, the Greek Edomites are still trying to take credit for the creation of the emblem, teaching us that the mythological Greek demigod of medicine, came up with the idea of a snake being placed upon a pole to heal the people. The truth is, Moses and the Israelites came along centuries before the mythological Greek demigod fairy tale even existed!

The Jewish

Through Abraham and Moses, the Jews (God's jewels), have a covenant with God. From the Jews the covenant has been extended to all the Hebrew nation without distinction. From the Israelites and Hebrews, the European Jewish nation of people originally descended from the Israelite tribes living in Canaan. Many of the other nations of people on Earth, especially the Edomites, envy the Jewish. By design, God created this nation of people above all other nations of people on the Earth. European Jews are the descendants of the Twelve Tribes of Israel, God's chosen nation of people. As a very important part of God's plan for them to be fruitful and multiply, it was the Lord's will that they ventured out from the Holy Land of Canaan and moved to Europe. By mingling with the Edomites in Europe, over time, they multiplied and became the European Jewish nation of God's people.

For higher purposes, the Lord has chosen the nation of Jewish people to be the wealthiest nation of people living here in the United States and in other parts of the world. Today, there are about fifteen million Jewish people worldwide and the majority of them reside in the United States and Israel. The God-given Jewish capitalism allows the Jewish people to own and control the majority of financial institutions, banks, and large companies across the United States. Jewish capitalism allows them to build the lavish synagogues throughout the world. Due to the royal blood flowing through their veins, they have always been envied by the Edomites, as well as by many other nations.

Being envious of the Jewish wealth and culture, the conflicts between Christianity and Judaism erupted and created anti-Semitism and hostility against the Jewish Nation. After the other nations became jealous of the Jewish nation of people the atmosphere of anti-Semitism against the Jews became prevalent. The hatred started first among the Edomites in Europe, then spread to other parts of the world.

Jewish Lives Matter

The lives of European Jewish people have always mattered! Knowing that the Jews are God's chosen people, out of envy, the German Edomites took anti-Semitism to the highest level possible. The Nazis believed that the German race of Edomites were superior to the Jewish nation of God's People. Just as White people in the United States of America felt that the Blacks and Israelites were nonhuman in their eyes, Adolf Hitler and the Nazi Klan felt that the Jewish people were nonhuman as well.

This mentality caused Adolf Hitler to say to the Nazis, "We are the superior race of people on Earth and will be doing the world a favor by wiping out the Jewish race." They believed that the precious lives of the Jewish people didn't matter. That's when the atrocious and heinous acts were carried out against God's Jewels by the German Edomites. The European Jews were then targeted for extermination. Hitler and his Klan would call it the Final Solution to the Jewish Question. It was discussed by the senior Nazi officials in January 1942, resulting in a written-out policy for the extermination of the Jewish population by the Nazis.

Because Jewish lives didn't matter to the German Edomites, about two thirds of the European Jewish population—six million (6,000,000 people) innocent men, women, and children—were murdered by the White German Edomites. By policy of extermination, the fugitives carried out the murders of God's Jewels by mass shootings, starvation, and gas chambers. Others were used as slaves and worked to death in concentration camps. Adolf Hitler and his Klan remain fugitives to this day awaiting

God's justice for the killings of His precious Jewels. The royal Jewish blood has cried out to the Lord, and justice for the senseless killings of the unarmed Jewish nation of God's people is at hand.

It's no coincidence that Jews are the majority of the population of people living in the Holy Land of Israel. It's the land that God has given to Abraham the founder of Judaism. The land has been inherited and cared for by the Jews for many generations. Israel is the Holy and original place of pilgrimage for the Jewish nation of people. They express their gratitude for inheriting the sacred soil through fervent prayer. Jewish people are the ones that go out of their way to make sure that God receives all the honor and praise due to Him.

Jewish people are on fire for God! What's not for God to love about His nation of people bowing down to Him with a prayer book in their hand, facing Mecca, and praying three times a day? His appointed people wake up each morning, zealously looking forward to prayer and communication with God the Father. The very thought of using a prayer book to pray with shows the great zeal of the Jewish people.

Depending on what's going on in their lives at any given time, a prescribed prayer is selected from the numerous prayers in the Siddurs. Just as a loving mother holds and rocks her infant child in her arms when it's time for sleep, the Chosen Ones hold scripture in their hands while rocking their upper bodies forward and back in a rhythmic sway as they recite their prayers to the Lord.

Being a Black Israelite, and a child of Baby boomers due to a covenant relationship with God, I was circumcised on Friday July 20, 1956. It was the eighth day of my life. Because the Jewish nation of people have a Covenant relationship with the Father, God gave the command of circumcision of every male child as mandatory. *"This is my covenant, which ye shall keep, between me and you and thy seed after thee; Every male child among you shall be circumcised. And ye shall circumcise the flesh of your foreskin; and it shall be a token of the covenant between me and you: And he that is eight days old shall be circumcised among you, every male child in your generations"* (Genesis 17:10–12).

Speaking of generations, because everything works in the moment, time and generations are important to God. All the generations in time have come to pass through intervals. Here in America our days begin at 12:00 a.m., midnight. Quite different from the way God created it to operate. With Jewish days beginning and ending at sundown, it shows us that the Jewish Israelites are the ones paying attention to how God structures time. The Lord spoke and said, "The evening and the morning were the first day." It's not intended to be the other way around. Not to mention the Edomites tampering with the Earth's rotation through Daylight Savings Time, which only caters to their own selfish agendas.

Out of respect for God's timing, the day always begins at sundown. The Jewish Israelites, especially the people living in Israel, obey the Lord as commanded. Also, they celebrate the weekly Sabbath day by resting. Because the Lord rested on the seventh day, every generation of Israelites are ordered by God to rest and observe His six-day completion of His Earth. It's a day that the Jewish nation dedicates to God, friends, and family. Therefore, in Israel, grocery shopping and the running of errands are taken care of in the other six days. On the seventh day, the Jewish nation of people obey God and do not go out to their favorite restaurant and pay for meals. Nor do they labor or work others.

Their ways are not like our ways here in America. When it comes to obeying God's word, there is a holy sensitivity among the European Jews. The Jewish community put their economy aside and show respect to the Lord and His economy. Buying and selling on the Sabbath day celebration is strictly prohibited by the Lord. Refer to Nehemiah 10:31. The Lord has the right to set the stipulations for His holy celebrations! Here in the United States, people have become desensitized to the harm that occurs from disobedience. At many mega churches across the US, items are sold at the church during the services. Church members are also accustomed to getting together and going out to eat at their favorite restaurants following church services. Americans have been desensitized to obeying God's word concerning the Sabbath.

Growing up, in America, a typical Sabbath day, even after church services would include me buying gasoline, and going to work. Many buy groceries and other items on the Lord's Holy Sabbath day of rest. The day is often used for house cleaning and yard work. Many of the Westerners use the Sabbath day for being intoxicated as they celebrate the movie stars and ball players for entertainment with their friends. The Lord's Sabbath day of rest has been turned into a day of recreation, entertainment, labor, and disrespect.

Chapter 7

Respecting God is Expected from God's Chosen.

God expects a lot more from the Israelites than He does from all other nations on Earth. Notice that He speaks directly to, and directly refers to the Children of Israel, six hundred and seventy-five (675) times throughout the Bible, signifying their importance to Him. The Lord spoke to the Israelites and said that the Sabbath day is a perpetual covenant between Him and the Israelites forever (Exodus 31:13–17). Therefore, the Sabbath day is established by God for the Israelites. His chosen nation of people are the ones responsible for honoring that day of rest.

On the other hand, the descendants of Esau, the Edomites, are mentioned only one hundred and four (104) times in the Bible.

The Edomites are spared from the Israelite's covenant with the Father. They do not have the same purpose and the same place in society as the Israelite Jews. God's chosen nation of people, having a deep admiration for the Lord, is the nation that He set aside to be the trendsetters in this world. Being determined to do things the way God has commanded us to do them, the main focus of the Israelites should be not to get caught up in the cultures of the Edomites and other nations.

The Animalistic Instinct in Us

No offense, but as people, let's face it, we are all animals originally created by God in the wilderness. Just as hyenas are the natural enemies to the lions, the Edomites are the natural enemies to the Israelites. In fact, the analogy between the two groups of animals forms a basis from which to consider them to be similar in their natural quest for survival. Being natural enemies, the Edomites are doing exactly what the Lord put them on the Earth to do. Their job is to persecute the Israelites until they have learned to obey God. As human beings, we must understand that we are animals, just like all other animals living on Earth. The difference is in our purpose.

In reference to Deuteronomy 7:7, the Lord chose the Israelite nation as His people because they were the fewest in number of all the other people on Earth. Like humans, all animals need the same things, mainly food, water, and shelter. Being relentless adversaries, hyenas outnumber the lions and use their larger population to control and compete for needed resources of survival. Likewise, the Edomites outnumbered the Israelites. They established their laws of disparity against the Israelites and used their mass population to unfairly compete with them for resources.

In the wilderness, the lions prides as well as the clans of hyenas all hunt on the same grounds. They are searching for the same prey, and scavenging the remains of other animals. Consequently, if the clan of hyenas outnumber the lions, they will kill and steal the food from the pride of lions. As the analogy goes on, the Edomites outnumbered the Israelites, murdered them and stole their native land Arsareth, and later renamed it America. Thus, becoming their stolen hunting grounds.

As in the competition between the lions and hyenas, the practice of the animals killing each other's young, leading to infanticide, makes it easier for animals to control a certain territory. This animalistic behavior introduces another observation of the existence of an analogy between the lions and hyenas verses the Israelites and the Edomites. For instance, Planned Parenthood, created by the White supremacist Margret Sanger, carried out a campaign of infanticide against the Israelites. Approximately nineteen million Black Israelite babies were aborted by the Edomite's organization. The lives of the baby Israelites did not matter to White supremacist or to the ignorant Black women who aborted them. Due to the infanticide, many Israelites were not procreated, making it easier for the Edomites to carry out their evil agenda here in America.

There is a secularist agenda in the American culture that seeks to change the way that Israelites feel about serving the Lord and avoiding covetousness.

Behind everything, there is a precise spiritual agenda. The Devil's plan is to take our mind off the Lord and put our daily focus on ways to accumulate more wealth and power. People in general are becoming more excited about gaining wealth and power than they are about doing God's will. The Lord looks at that mentality and deals with it accordingly.

Remember, God deals with nations. As more Israelites today are being caught up in the American ways by putting the desire to accumulate wealth in front of daily obedience to God's word, it causes the Israelites to suffer as a nation. When God's chosen speak more often of their selfish desires of winning lotteries and receiving gifts, in oppose to doing the things that are pleasing to God, it displeases Him. The Lord wants His chosen ones to trust that He will supply all of their daily needs in life. When people trust in the Lord, that's the best way of acknowledging God's divine agenda of taking care of all of His children.

Knowing where their blessings are going to come from, the Children of Israel should not worry about money. They should fully trust that God the Father will supply all of their needs. We all know that when it comes to having daily conversations with people, we have a tendency to talk to people about the things that we love and trust. We talk about what's most important to us at the time. However, when we choose to ramble on about the desire of financial gain, in oppose to talking about what we are doing to please the Lord, our agenda is transparent to Him, and the love of money pushes us away from the love of God. At the same time, it pulls us in the direction of covetousness and stinginess.

Having a large abundance of money and not being willing to share with those in need is one of the ungodly signs of greed. The more money that a rich person has, the more they seem to want. Money can become an idol and a false god in the American culture. As it corrupts the mind, money has become a false god to many. The Lord has said in His word multiple times that money (mammon) turns a person's heart away from Him. Just like it happened to King Solomon, it could happen to anyone. *"But lay up for yourselves treasures in heaven, where nei-*

ther moth nor rust doth corrupt, and where thieves do not break through nor steal: For where your treasure is, there will your heart be also" (Matthew 6:20–21).

Accumulating wealth and power has always been the American way for Edomites. However, over a period of time, materialism has seriously corroded the American society. For the sake of greediness, it became customary for Edomite business owners to begin working on the Sabbath day of the Lord for financial gain. Happening reluctantly, the Israelites have been dragged into this culture of greediness. The Israelites were taken as slave captives and shipped to work in a society of people that thrives on materialism.

Edomites knowing that in the Israelite culture the Sabbath day is set aside as a day of rest, forced the Israelites to disobey God. The money-grabbing business owners would force the Israelites to work on the Sabbath or have the option of losing their family income. The Israelites were forced under extreme duress to work on the Sabbath. Consequently, working on the Sabbath day has desensitized Israelites to

God's commandment of them to this very day.

Exchanging God for Secular Entertainment

On a different note, the mind has become desensitized to the dangers of secular entertainment. By people being addicted to worldly amusement, God gets neglected. When the Lord gets neglected, society gets neglected. Seeking and being a part of worldly amusement leads to worldliness. Society in general is devoted to seeking recreation for escapism, but it comes with a hefty price tag. The deadly vice of worldly distractions becomes compulsive and interferes with the relationship that the Lord has with His people.

Can we afford to have our personal relationship with the Lord weakened? The consequences for self-indulgence and trying to escape God's sacred reality through amusement are merited. Loving entertainment, in oppose to loving God with all your heart, soul, and mind is sabotage. In a different light, the Lord and His angels also need to be entertained. The thought may have never entered your mind, but the only way to entertain the Lord is to worship Him. Since societies worldwide has chosen to worship money and amusement, the Lord has to find ways to get the attention of His people.

Getting the world's attention comes easily for the Lord. In today's society beginning in the year 2020, consequences for worshiping false idols emerged as the Lord sent His plague of Covid-19 throughout civilization. Not only that, the Lord quickly brought public leisure and entertainment to a halt. The all-seeing God has reformed entertainment. It's the year of death. Today's general population is being entertained by seeing people walking around with funny-looking masks covering their faces out of the fear of becoming sick and dying alone. The population has become amused at seeing thousands get sick daily and dying from Covid-19. By October of the year 2020, one million people worldwide had died from the coronavirus. Due to worldwide sickness and death, many people were banned from going to work. When income is limited, and families have to spend their life savings just to survive, their perspective changes. Money is no longer viewed as their god. It becomes a necessity. That's when people start praying for God's help.

Police killings of unarmed Israelites has come to light, and is seen on national television worldwide, sparking the new civil rights movement globally. This new type of entertainment snowballed into the Israelites and other nations viewing the coming to light of racial disparities. Regular social activities such as tearing down and removing Confederate monuments has become the new subjects of entertainment for television. All new television shows and movies are suspended due to the coronavirus. The old boring reruns are the new normal for television shows. Due to the prominence of racism in the US, people are becoming amused at seeing mixed races of people marching in the streets for racial equality and justice for all.

Just for fun, widespread street recreation in the form of rioting, looting, and arson has become the new normal. Millions of people are living it up, after filing for unemployment and being paid four times the money to stay at home and entertain themselves. For the amusement of the president of the United States and government officials, monies have to be forked out to businesses and millions of people to balance the economy. In sports entertainment, the players are now forced to play and earn their money without the glory of a live audience praising and cheering them on. Just for the sport of it, team owners now have to honor multimillion-dollar contracts to professional sports players without ticket sales creating profits for stadiums and arenas.

With crowd restriction laws in place, limiting gatherings to ten people or less, to my surprise, church services are being held either in the parking lot or online across the United States. That makes it harder to pass the collection plate around. The Lord doesn't want or need your money anyway. The minister and your family does. Having to do without the multimillion-dollar incomes from weekly offerings funded by church members, the dire need for government assistance arises. Being faith-based organizations here in the United States, churches are eligible to receive Small Business Association (SBA) loans. The federal government is now having to provide money directly to churches paying for pastor's salaries and utility bills. The average salary of the mega church minister is only $147,000 annually.

The God of This World

With Satan being the all-experienced god of this world, he understands the behavior and psychology of humankind. He uses money as well as entertainment as vehicles to distract and deceive the majority of people from the things that God has promised. As a social normalcy, the lifetimes of many people were spent focused on Satan's many vehicles of endless entertainment. The other group of people focus was on money, power, and controlling the poor. At any rate, people don't want to admit that spending a lifetime focusing on things that does not matter at the end of one's life is rigorously pursuing the hidden agenda of Satan.

Through money (mammon), Satan sets out to challenge God's agenda. Being in place first, the Lord's agenda is the covenant He made with the Children of Israel. However, with their priorities bent, the majority of nations, including the Israelites, has placed their hopes in currency and the things money can bring as opposed to God and the things He has to offer, which are priceless. Hiding the truth from the Israelites is the priority of the Edomites as well as being Satan's deceptive agenda.

The primary truth that has been hidden from God's Chosen in the United States is who they are in relation to who Jesus the Son of God is. The blindness that has been established among the masses of the Israelites by the Edomites has kept them from bonding together as the stronger nation of people. Viewed by Whites as the weakest, the Israelites have always felt inferior to the Edomites because of bywords and slavery. The inferiority complex has further been established by Satan through media and currency. The media has always portrayed the Blacks as being less intelligent and more violent than Whites.

Look at the predominately White people over Blacks whom hold the offices in the Senate and Congress. Sadly, 95 percent of the Supreme Court justices have been White men. Out of forty-five presidents of the United States, forty-three were White Edomite men and only two were Israelite Black men. Ninety-seven percent of all Republican elected officials are White. This is because the elite Whites already have the money, and they are more concerned about profits than the welfare of the people. The Whites are the ones that make the important laws that run this country. The Blacks are seen predominantly playing children's ball games in sports, singing and dancing while the Edomite White men run the country.

The media influences the world philosophies. In general, Black families don't have as much money as the White families. The fact is, people controlling the United States currency and media has always had a major influence on the ideas, opinions, education, and commerce in the United States culture. Over the years, being educated by Edomites, the Israelites have been constantly lied to in order to keep them from knowing the truth about how important they are to God and what the Lord expects of them. Israelites should be the ones establishing the laws and running this country. After all, the 3.8 million square miles of land stolen by the Edomites, and renamed the United States of America belonged to the Israelites in the first place.

The original owners of this land should have been the ones making the laws in this country. The alien Edomite nation of people should have been the ones being praised for being the best at professionally playing sports, while the Israelites were establishing the laws of the land. The Edomites should have been the ones being praised for singing and dancing around the Israelites while the people of color were establishing and enforcing the original Arsareth laws and culture. They should have built up their own 3.8 million square miles of land. Having land snatched away from the Israelites by Edomites were some of the darkest times in history. It dramatically changed the course of the future of God's Chosen, the Israelite nation.

The uprising of a seventy-year-old propaganda campaign has returned and is being repeated in the United States under a different name. The first civil rights crusade began in the late 1940s and ended in the late 1960s. Many decades ago, the civil rights activist Reverend Dr. Martin Luther King Jr. led the Civil Rights Project to end racial discrimination and gain equal rights under the law. Unwilling to promote change, the plan of the Edomites was to crucify the leader and watch the followers succumb. It almost happened. The movement slowed with King's assassination by the Edomites.

Black Lives Matter Movement

The time has come when history repeats itself under the new name, Black Lives Matter. Beware of the equal rights propaganda being shoved down your throat. Does it really take over seventy years for equal rights laws to go into effect? The upcoming generations are new to the ways of the world and are having trouble differentiating between truth and propaganda. I have lived through the '50s and '60s and heard it all before. Yea, Black lives matter to God and the Israelites, but they do not matter to the masses of Edomites running this country. If Black lives mattered, after the assassination of Reverend Dr. Martin Luther King Jr., equal rights laws would have gone into effect decades ago.

Instead, thousands of more Israelites with the same skin complexion were assassinated by Edomite police officers on many streets named Dr. Martin Luther King Jr. Boulevard. To his dishonor, so far nothing has changed to rectify the problems. Biblically speaking, the true way of saying Black Lives Matter would be by saying, Israelite Lives Matter. If Israelites lives really mattered to the Edomites, they would change the laws of justice and do the right thing. Don't hold your breath waiting for change. The only way for the Whites to even begin to right the wrongs that were done to the Israelites would be to give back the 3.8 million miles of land stolen from them. What are the chances of that happening?

It would be the right thing to do! There should be no statute of limitations for righting the wrongs in reference to the known history of racial discrimination and disparities placed upon the Israelites. The pending public relation issues of Black Lives Matter merits reason for the leaders of this country to hold a national press conference. Over the past seventy years, we should have been seeing daily press conferences addressing the changes that had taken place in the laws for racial equality. It never happened then, and is unlikely to happen now. It's because to the leaders of this country, systemic racism, and disparities of the people of color does not matter. So the Black Lives Matter propaganda as seen on television advertised by the Edomites' media will amount to nothing. Unfortunately, as the generations come and go, things will remain as they are.

Think about it, put yourself in the shoes of the Edomites, White people. They look at it this way: they do not want people of color to have as much or even more than they do. Would you put yourself in the position to have to start over financially, by giving back the land that your ancestors had stolen from someone else, and had given it to you and to your families? After being in complete control of running a country the way you want it ran, catering to the needs of your own people, and having the option of being or not being concerned with the welfare of others, would you suddenly change your laws and put yourself in a position of losing control of money and power? I think not!

We must realize that we are not living in a Do-the-right-ethical-thing world. In fact, it's quite the opposite. We live in a world where unethical laws were established by the Whites and honored as the laws of the land. Few people have researched the root cause of racial disparities here in Arsareth/America. The birth of racial disparities began with the stolen land of Arsareth. When Israelites owned the land, they had the upper hand from the beginning. The land that God had given them made them the front runners. Things changed very quickly.

After the Edomites had murdered thousands of Israelite men, women, and children, and took their land, they gained the upper hand. You see, since Black lives did not matter to them in the year 1492 when the White men killed the Israelites and took their land, what makes you think Black lives matter now? Another example of bringing disparities upon the Israelites by taking away their property occurred in Tulsa, Oklahoma. It was the Greenwood Massacre that took place in the spring of 1921. The senseless murders of the Israelites happened because White citizens were outraged at the fact that Black citizens were doing well and running their own businesses on what they referred to as Black Wall Street.

The Greenwood Massacre led by mobs of mostly deputized White supremacists were given weapons by city and state officials to kill the Black residents and destroy their property. The killings and destruction started on May 31 and ended on June 1, leaving three hundred Black residents dead and their properties destroyed, which brought disparities upon their future generations. Inequalities among the Blacks will remain because the Edomites established unjust laws that over the years have solidified racial disparities here in Arsareth/America, the homeland of the Israelites.

Take a look at the multimillion-dollar skyscrapers in the cities across the US.

The organizations of people owning these buildings couldn't care less about racial disparities. Regardless of how Edomites came to own the tall structures, they belong to them now. So the Israelites don't merit the right nor have the means to take existing structures from the Edomites. Even though they unjustly took the land Arsareth from the Israelites, whose lives did not matter to them, the Edomites still built their structures and renamed the Israelites homeland, the United States of America. As of the year 2020, it's been over five hundred years since the senseless murders of the ten tribes of Israel at the bloody hands of White men. It would be hard to teach an old dog new tricks.

The Edomite nation of people are now set in their ways. How can anyone believe, by any stretch of their imagination, that Black lives matter to the United States government or justice system? The equal rights propaganda being broadcast by US media is a double-dealing hoax. The propagandist knows that the pulling down of White supremacist monuments doesn't change any of the laws regarding racial disparities.

It may hurt your feelings, but it's like shoving a pacifier in the mouth of a screaming baby that's wanting milk. The child knows the difference between hot air and milk. People talking about racial disparities are only blowing hot air out of their mouths. Who needs a pacifier? What people need is for laws to be reformed to implement changes. Changes in American laws are needed to eradicate racism and racial disparities. When it comes to racial injustices, modern history shows that politicians and lawmakers are very articulate at talking their talk. Yet they have no clout, when it comes to walking the walk of justice.

As you wait patiently for equal rights to change in the law, your children will have grown into adults. Present time would have turned into decades. You are now enjoying the life of being a grandparent to your grandchildren. To your surprise, you see that no lasting changes are made. More promises are being made by the government. On media broadcast, political leaders are still explaining why racial disparities have worsened over the years. The new generation of protesters begin to organize street marches. "Déjà vu." In hindsight, you learn how to spot propaganda.

Edomites never had and never will have intentions of giving the Israelites equal rights or fair justice. Here in Arsareth/America, when the leaders plan on getting things done, they are addressed in a National Press Conference. When did the president of the United States ever hold a press conference addressing racial injustices and disparities? It's not happening in America. Israelites putting their trust in a media that's owned by a nation of people that the Lord sent against them, says a lot about their character.

If Israelites had obeyed God and took His word seriously, we would not be in this predicament in the first place. No one and no laws can change what the Lord has purposed in His will. However, because the Israelites disobeyed God, He purposed the Edomites to establish their laws to work against us. *"Therefore shalt thou serve thine enemies which the Lord shall send against thee, in hunger and thirst, and in nakedness, and in want of things; and he shall put a yoke of iron upon thy neck, until he have destroyed thee"* (Deuteronomy 28:48).

Today's Modernized Slavery

From the plantation into modernized slavery, the word prevails. Today's Israelites here in the United States are a destroyed nation of people serving their enemies which the Lord sent against them. In today's era, Israelites are serving the Edomites in their workplace for an agreed payment for their services. You may call it what you'd like. Our modern-day slave numbers are actually our social security numbers. The yoke of iron (wage inequality) represents the ownership of the slaves. Disparities today may be seen as Israelites in want of things that the other nation of people (the Edomites) possess.

What does the Edomites possess that we want? Let's begin with the primary necessity of food. Are we in want of food? The White man owns the major food chains across America. The majority of the Israelites have to go to the Edomites to keep food on the table for their families. The water supply is owned by the Edomites. Who can live without water? Power plants producing electricity and natural gas are owned by the Edomites. If you don't serve them in order to make a living, you have no money to pay them for supplying your family with electricity. Here in America, when you need gasoline for your vehicle, the White man controls the supply here in, and coming into, the US. The list goes on and on.

So you feel that because you started a business you don't fit into the category of slave... Being people of color, it's mandatory that we pay the cost of city and state licenses to another nation of people in order to legally run a business. You have to register with the White man's taxing authorities. Your business operation license, doing business as permits, and federal employer identification numbers are distributed by the US government. Through zoning laws, the Edomites determine where you can legally run a business. If you don't pay your taxes to them on time, the Edomites will snatch your business right out of your hands immediately. There would be nothing you could do to stop them. We need their okay and stamp of approval on almost everything we do. Remember that the White man pays his taxes to his own nation of people, while the Israelites pay their taxes to whom God calls our enemy.

Also, keep in mind that God is the ruler over all the nations. Things are quickly changing and there is light at the end of the tunnel for God's Chosen Israelites. Everything that's happening today is leading up to unimaginable events to take place in the near future. The Lord has the last word in all of this. Even though the Lord is using the nation of Edomites to chastise the Israelites, He has orchestrated an intricate plan of judgment against that nation. It's through international orchestration that the Lord will overthrow the Edomites opposing the Israelites here in America.

So you ask me, "Exactly how is God going to have the Edomites overthrown?" That's not meant to be known. The answer to that question is beyond our perception. The Lord's strategic plan of overthrowing the Edomites is hush-hush and beyond our scrutiny. His well-timed actions to overthrow the Edomites are hidden out of sight and out of mind. His actions may be in plain view, yet beyond our perception. As far as we know, COVID-19 could be a part of God's arsenal for His warfare. However, for the sake of justice for the Israelites, God is working nationally and internationally and His operations are certain. His intervention on behalf of His Chosen Ones is sure. Everything will happen in its time. Before the conception of time as we know it, the Lord had already orchestrated the overthrowing of the Edomites. He is coming to the rescue of His Chosen nation of people. We must all prepare ourselves now. Our God doesn't sit on the Throne planning His next move. He just waits on His calendar day that's already established. *"But, beloved, be not ignorant of this one thing, that one day is with the Lord is a thousand years, and a thousand years as one day. The Lord is not slack concerning His promise, as some men count slackness: but is longsuffering to us, not willing that any should perish but that all should come to repentance"* (2 Peter 3:8–9).

When the time comes, salvation requires repentance on the part of all nations including the nation of Edomites. Everyone has to own up to their transgressions before the unknown scheduled date. For efficient spiritual warfare, the startle effect is a vital tactic used by God. That's why Jesus said, "No one knows the time or the date, not even the angels in Heaven or Him." The element of surprise works effectively against hypocrisy and deceit which comes under the judgment of God. Being caught napping, not repenting for our transgressions would be eternally catastrophe.

Repentance of a Nation

Just as God was remorseful about creating man in His image, remorsefulness is commanded of us for our sins. The Lord Himself owned up to the responsibility of his feelings of wrong doing by creating man in His Holy image. *"And it repented the Lord that He made man on the earth, and it grieved Him at His heart. And the Lord said, I will destroy man whom I have created from the face of the Earth; both man and beast, and the creeping thing, and the fowls of the air; for it repented me that I have made them"* (Genesis 6:6–7). Since God, being the Creator of the universe, owns up to His responsibility by repenting, who are we to not feel obligated to repent for our wrong doing? The fact is we, as human beings, are liable and held accountable for our sins. Most importantly, we can only prove our innocence to God by repenting, as the Lord has done.

As a nation, the central goal in life should be to love the Lord with all our heart, soul, and mind. When it comes to interpersonal relationships, the Lord is paying attention to the way we feel and behave toward each other. By God comprehending that we all know what's right and what's wrong, we are all under obligation to repent for the ill treatment of everyone we have come in contact with our entire lives. This applies to each individual person that's ever walked the Earth.

As a nation of people, the Edomites have always had strained relationships with the Israelites. It is sufficient here to reiterate that the Israelites were kidnapped, enslaved, demoralized, as well as stripped of their homeland Arsareth, by the Edomites. God delivered the Israelites into the hands of their enemies only to serve them. The Lord did not give the Edomites the license to undermine His people, and the White man's selfish ambition and extreme cruelty toward the Israelites was unhallowed. In fact, serving does not include being whipped, raped, killed, having their children taken, and separated from their families. These atrocious and heinous acts will require repentance from all parties connected with enslaving and demoralizing the families of Israelites. All nations involved with the disparities of the Israelites are under God's obligation to repent for their deeds from past generations to the present.

Failed Public Relations

Headed by the United States Federal Government, the American Law Institute (ALU) and the Uniform Law Commission (ULC) are responsible for creating new laws and adjustments to fix and eliminate the disparities of the Israelite Nation of people living here in Arsareth/America. Acknowledging the dilemmas and being remorseful of the present malpractices would be the first step to accomplishing changes in the laws. The road that leads to new developments in legislation has been blocked, because the National Conference of Commissioners on uniform state laws are working against the people of color.

How are public relation issues addressed and resolved in America? The first stage would be a press conference! Here in America, when public relation issues in society need to be addressed, the sitting president holds a national press conference. It's been over a hundred years since Woodrow Wilson held the first presidential press conference. Since the Wilson Administration, sixteen successors have held hundreds of press conferences and not once have a press conference been held on the public relation issues of systemic racism and racial disparities.

The United States was alerted many years back on the public relation issues of systemic racism and racial disparities. These are national emergencies that merit the need of having national press conferences. As already seen in the past hundred years, all the interviews with journalist and reporters are proven to have been useless. Addressing the issue is a nice gesture, but when things remain as they are, what's the use? Gaining coverage in newspapers, magazines, blogs, and news broadcasts doesn't get any laws revised. For laws to be changed, Israelite Jews will need the support of state and national legislators.

The difficulty lies in the fact that the goals of the state and federal legislators are keeping the people of color poor. Systemic racism and racial disparities are not issues that state and federal legislators are willing to pursue. These public relation issues are old, not new. The ideological spectrum of predominately White conservative and liberal legislators are prioritizing all other issues of law over systemic racism and racial disparities. We are aware that changing laws takes time, but centuries have come and gone waiting for lawmakers to take action. As previously experienced, it will take many more centuries for the laws of systemic racism and racial disparities to even be voted upon and defeated by the Edomites.

It's very unlikely that laws will change because they are upholding and reflecting the values and beliefs of the White race. In other words, racism and racial disparities to the White people in charge are not relevant public relation issues. As in the past, the Edomite presidents of the United States did not, and are not going to, modify the Constitution to benefit Black people. Why? Because it would be inconsistent with the Constitution itself. Political parties are not on your side if you are representing people of color. Maybe if the federal courts had a sudden change of heart... I think not!

You may say, he's just being pessimistic, but history teaches us differently. Check the house dockets for yourself. You think state and national legislators are going to support Israelites? Go ahead and file your referendum for establishing the laws that would abolish systemic racism and racial disparities among the Israelites. You can start by gathering signatures and filing your intention to have it placed on the next available ballot. Present your argument. Actually, you have no argument to present because the arguments have already been presented to the United States legislators and lawmakers many years ago. Go ahead and use the "Necessary and Proper" clause of the United States Constitution for eliminating systemic racism and racial disparities and see where it gets you. Well, we can always look at the bright side, at least you don't have to sit at the back on the bus anymore. That's about the only thing that has changed—overt racism.

Even though it's not relevant to the Edomites, major changes in public relation laws are necessary in order to do away with systemic racism and racial disparities. For the Israelites, slavery and George Floyd's death are pivotal points in history when laws were in dire need of change for the sake of future generations. Addressing social unfairness issues and not following up on them as done in the past will forever be inadequate for the Israelites in America. We sing the old spiritual, "A Change is Gonna Come," but when?

Chapter 8

God's Justice for All

Looming just over the horizon, the day is coming when the Lord gathers all of His children in His arms. The trumpet sounds. God's justice overrides all injustices in the Lord's moral government. At last, institutionalized injustice can no longer stand in the way of justice. Unfairness will be abolished from the world. The Lord deeply cares for the people that have repented for all their sins and has accepted Jesus Christ as their personal Savior. Whether you be an Edomite, Israelite, Moabite, Ammonite, or any other nation of people, your relationship with God, determines your eternal fate. Morally right and justifiable in accordance with the Lord's Divine Law, fairness is everyone's God-given right and is extended to all equally with love.

God's justice for all is the way He shows love. The fair treatment of all the nations is His desired goal. When all the nations have become one, prejudice is eliminated. As nations, we deserve to know what it feels like to live in unison, one with the other. The color of skin and texture of hair should not determine how a person is to be treated. As humans, we all have skin that serves the same purpose. Some people have more hair than others, but the length and color does not determine how one is to be treated. Hair grows out of the skin and all skin tones are created equal.

God causes it to rain on the just as well as the unjust, and it is His will that no man shall perish, and we all shall have eternal life. All nations of the world are truly loved by the Creator, and He wants us to love others as He loves us. In order for us to do that, we have to learn to forgive as God forgives, without a spot or wrinkle. Don't spend so much time trying to figure out if you should forgive a person. Just do it! Forgiveness is not for the person that sinned against you. It's for you. The Lord could have already forgiven the people that you're hating, and when He comes, you will be judged for hating them. What good is that going to do you? Keeping hatred in check is vital for salvation.

It's our duty to love everyone and give them their due. It's not in our jurisdiction to punish anyone. The Bible says that vengeance is the Lord's. Only He is just to render harsh punishment upon His people. We have a tendency to treat people as if they were property and we own them. I own my cell phone. Destroying my cell phone by tossing it in the river is one thing, but throwing a human being in the river is quite different. I may have owned that cell phone, but no one can actually own another person. They don't have a Heaven or a Hell to place your spirit in after the Judgment. Because the Lord owns all human beings; everyone must be treated with respect and dignity.

The Lord's fair treatment toward all people is beyond our reasoning. The actions taken by the Lord rendering His justice goes beyond any type of scrutiny, whether it be men, or whether it be angels. No one can question God's ways. What type of fool would demand to hear the reasons for God doing the things He does for justice? Who would know of a better way of obtaining fairness than God Himself? *"For my thoughts are not your thoughts, neither are your ways my ways, saith the Lord. For as the heavens are higher than the Earth, so are my ways higher than your ways, and my thoughts than your thoughts"* (Isaiah 55:8–9).

We will never understand how God operates in the realm of holiness and fairness. However, just as we parents feel for our children, the Lord also feels for His children. He wants all nations alike to feel His love shining down upon us at all times. Nations coming together is the work of the Lord. On the other hand, when nations of people are being divided, it's the work of Satan. The Lord is relentlessly working to bring all the nations of the world together. God always operates from a point of love. For instance, out of love, as bad as it may seem, the international plague known as COVID-19 is a vehicle that God is using to bring all the nations of people together. It's also used as a vehicle to quickly bring many of His Children home to Him. Over a million souls have returned to God by way of the coronavirus.

The Father and His angels are celebrating the deaths caused by the plague. Nothing is more fulfilling to the Father than bringing His children home to safety. The Bible teaches us that we should celebrate the death of people and mourn the birth of our children. Being human, we are all guilty of doing just the opposite. People don't appreciate the irony of being happy when a loved one dies, and being sad when children are born. Not only does COVID-19 bring families together in Heaven, it also brings families together here on Earth. Having to distance ourselves from family for the sake of good health, people are missing and appreciating their family members more than ever before. As humans, we miss the element of touch. The young have to make sure that the elderly have what is needed during the crisis.

Not being discriminatory, COVID-19 teaches us a valuable lesson on being prejudice. Since the disease does not discriminate and effects all races of people, no one race can be singled out. Say for instance, if the disease only attacked the White race of people, history teaches that another race of people could rise up and feel superior over the Whites, and commit genocide against them. The Lord could have caused the disease to affect only a certain race. With the Lord knowing the outcome and mentality of humans, and loving all the different nations of people He created, He chose not to target a specific nation of people with the plague.

The Lord is the God of fairness, giving all nations a fair shake off the limb of the disease that we call the Corona virus. Because the virus has become the common enemy to all nations, nationally and internationally, we are forced to learn new ways of uniting the people in the medical field worldwide for one common cause. So the World Health Organization jumps on the bandwagon helping to create a vaccine to successfully subdue the virus.

The Lord is testing the faith of all nations by allowing us to go through this pandemic. He needs to know where our faith and hearts truly are. God is expecting us to find joy in everything that He does. That would include Him sending His plague throughout the world. Being the one in control, He wants us to look to Him for problem-solving before connecting with other nations to solve our dilemmas. When putting God first, two heads are better than one. Meaning God's and ours. The problem lies with the leaders of countries not acknowledging God. However, when nations come together and work alongside each other during a worldwide health crisis, it's pleasing in the sight of the Lord.

Caring enough to work together while helping one another demonstrates the ability of different societies to agree and come together as one. There is still a trust issue among the nations. For instance, if Russia comes up with a vaccine first, the United States government would not trust them enough to use the vaccine in the US. Neither would Russia trust the United States if the situation was reversed. History shows us that after becoming enemies following World War II, the United States would no longer share the Russians' best interest. Would it even be wise for a republic country like Arsareth/America to trust a

Communist society like Russia? With both countries being ideologically divided, conflicts between the two could be a disaster.

As ruler over the nations, God's global operation shall prevail over mankind. Hidden from human perception is the Lord's plan for things to come. Just as we could never have imagined the state of the world being as it is today, no one could ever know what tomorrow will bring. That's why the Lord says in His word to not boast about your plans for tomorrow. In reference to what's going on in the present world today, as far as we know, the Lord could have purposed scientists to create a virus that would spread all over the world.

If that were the case, the Lord's ulterior motive would not be the same as man's. Mankind (governments) want to dethrone God and rule the world, but overpopulated countries present a major obstacle. The problem could be that there are too many people in the world. So a mad scientist at the direction of secret societies could have created the virus in a laboratory. To rectify the problem of an over populated world, COVID-19 would be the most efficient method of killing masses of people worldwide.

The Great Deception

Here is a hypothetical scenario of how things could happen. With the general population being oblivious to what's happening as they are focused on the civil rights movement, earning money, and entertainment, a secret society, concealing their existence may have secretly planned a massive extermination of the general public. Sworn to secrecy, scientist may be guilty of creating the virus that is now spreading throughout the world. It's the perfect storm.

As people are falling victim to the new virus, cities and states worldwide are forced to shut down. Businesses are closed, forcing the general public out of work. Over a thousand people a day are dying in the United States alone. With the seasons changing into fall approaching winter, the number dramatically increases. Hospitals have become severely overwhelmed. To everyone's surprise, government spending becomes overwhelmed as leaders try and save their economies. Governments worldwide are becoming bankrupt. The world economy is on the verge of collapse. The stock market crashes. Global wealth is being dissolved as world currencies are declining and failing. People are desperate and succumbing to the virus in larger numbers nationwide.

The president, doctors, and leaders around the world start announcing through press conferences that a vaccine is now available that promises to prevent the virus. Millions of people are taking the vaccine unaware of its side effects. A few months go by and suddenly millions of people all at once become deathly ill. People, young and old, soon begin falling dead in the streets globally. The explanation now given to the people in press conferences is that the virus has mutated and doctors don't know how to treat it. The masses of people that did not take the vaccine are still susceptible to the original virus, but are unscathed by the so-called virus mutation.

Another dilemma arises adding to the desperation of the people. The worst is yet to come as malnourishment plagues families due to inadequate diets. Our children are dying from starvation. Fresh foods are becoming more difficult to come by, causing world hunger and more health problems arise globally. Money is useless to the New World Economy. The world changes as governments are forced to merge into One World Government. Society has now reached the pivotal point. The Lord allows Satan to startup his new economy.

The New World Communist Government is demanding that everyone receives a traceable human microchip implant in their right hand or forehead. The government-issued microchip implant is linked to the government's external database computer that identifies everyone with a personal ID number, economic history, and medical records. The only way anyone can participate in the new economy is through the human microchip implant. Prophecy has now come to pass. *"And he caused all, both small and great, rich and poor, free and bond, to receive a mark in their right hand, or in their foreheads. And that no man might buy or sell, save he that had the mark, or the name of the beast, or the number of his name"* (Revelation 13:16–17).

The time will come when the world will be deceived through technology. Happening in real time, right now the government has classified technology that's been hidden from society. These unknown technologies of deception are designed to deceive great masses of people all at once. Holograms may be used as vehicles of deception. For those unfamiliar with holograms they are physical recordings that reproduce three dimensional light fields that result in an image that retains the depth, parallax, and other properties of a recorded scene.

The Edomites have spent many millions of dollars setting their nest among the stars. Orbiting only 220 miles above the Earth is the International Space Station. With the right technology, signals can be transmitted from the ISS and produce advanced holograms. Don't be fooled. Just like your cell phone transmits signals across the globe at the speed of light, signals producing advanced holograms can be transmitted from the ISS as well. It's possible that through advanced holograms, secret societies are foolishly planning to overthrow Christianity. *"And he doeth great wonders, so that he maketh fire come down from heaven on the earth in the sight of men. And he deceiveth them that dwell on the Earth by the means of those miracles which he had power to do in the sight of the beast; saying to them that dwell on the Earth, that they should make an image to the beast, which had the wound by a sword, and did live"* (Revelation 13:13–14).

Advanced holograms sent to Earth by secret societies could easily deceive the very elect. With features like temperature, smell, sound, and a combination of other technologies, the advanced hologram recordings being sent down to Earth could cause people to fall down and worship the beast. The International Space Station may be new to us, but the Prophet Obadiah wrote about it in The Old Testament thousands of years ago.

Once the prophecy has been fulfilled, the International Space Station transmitting its advanced holograms of deception will suddenly be brought down to the Earth by the Lord. *"Though thou exalt thyself as the eagle, and though thou set thou nest among the stars, thence will I bring thee down, saith the Lord"* (Obadiah 1:4). Here in the Scriptures, the Lord speaks of Edomites in America exalting themselves as the eagle. The main vehicle that the Edomites uses to exalt themselves is their MONEY.

The bald eagle is the national emblem of the United States of America. The eagle is presented on the back of the Edomites gold coins, silver dollars, half dollars, and quarters with outspread wings. American money is blood money. It was created and built upon the stolen land that was taken from the Israelites through murder. The Lord's prophecy spoken to Obadiah pronounces the judgment of God against the Edomites for their past and present ill treatment of the Israelites. The acts of murdering the Israelites, stealing their land, and claiming it as their own, will never set well with the Most High God.

For those not familiar with the word *confederacy*, it's defined as an organization of people gathered together for unlawful purposes. The confederacy are the massive groups of Edomites that fought to keep the

Israelites enslaved here in the Arsareth/America, the native land of the Israelites. What does God say about the confederacy? *"And the men of thy confederacy have brought thee even to the border: the men that were at peace with thee have deceived thee; they that eat thou bread have laid a wound under thee: there is none understanding in him. Shall I not in that day, saith the Lord, even destroy the wise men out of Edom, and understanding out of the mount of Esau?"* (Obadiah 1:7–8).

We can see that the Lord greatly despises the confederacy. The confederacy has always been offensive toward the Israelites, treating them like wild animals. There is a lot to be learned concerning how God expects humans to be treated. One of the primary reasons that God created animals was to teach mankind the proper ways of having dominion over other things. It all started in the Garden of Eden when the Lord paraded all the animals in front of Adam giving him the responsibility of naming them.

Before the Lord created woman, the animals were Adam's first responsibility. Adam took on the responsibility, obeyed the Lord and gave names to all the animals in the Garden. It's safe to say that even though he had dominion over them, he was not cruel toward them. Likewise, the animals were never violent toward him. Neither were they violent toward each other. The Bible also states that the serpent was the only animal in the garden having the ability to speak. The peaceful animals were all setting an example of love toward one another. While naming the male and female pairs of animals, Adam was learning a lesson about love.

By Adam observing all the different animals getting along in the Garden, it was easier for him to reflect love in his character when God brought his companion to him: Adam named his wife Eve, and the Lord gave Adam and Eve dominion over all of the animals that He had created. In the Lord's eyes, having dominion over animals did not imply violence or mistreatment of the animals. It meant taking care of God's animals and being a good steward over them. The animals belonged to God, not to Adam.

The same golden rule applies to people when having dominion over other people. When people are sent to serve other people, the ones that are being served are never entitled to inflict violence or mistreat the servant. When the Lord gives us rule or power over someone, we must realize that people are the property of God, not the property of human beings. The rulers of nations are to be good stewards over the people.

Truth versus Opinions

Everyone has opinions except for God. Humans have their opinions about the infallibility of God's Word. I can confidently say that the Bible and prophecy are, in fact, authentic. Being that the Lord knows the whole truth about everything, opinions are foolish and serves the Lord no purpose. Every other being has their own opinions about something, because no one but the Lord knows everything. The truth is that human beings are created by God to serve Him. An example of an assumption of that truth by an atheist would be: there is no God.

People seem to have their own assessments on whether or not the Bible stands as the truth. Opinions are based upon foolish beliefs that fall short of certainty. As stated by the Bible, *"The fool hath said in his heart, there is no God. They are corrupt, they have done abominable works, there is none that doeth good"* (Psalms 14:1). From this statement, the atheist point of view concerning this truth would be, there is no God and human beings are not obligated to serve God. However, truth will always trump over assumptions. The truth is, there is a higher power over humanity. The atheistic opinion of that would be that man created himself, either before or after the universe created itself.

When it comes to truth versus opinion, it would be accurate to say that humans can't physically live without air to breath or water to drink. However, people have a right to form their thesis before they die from the lack of air and water. Our opinions aren't worth anything to God. The truth is all that matters to Him. As for the nations, the Lord said in His word (Deuteronomy 7:6) that the nation of Israelites are His Chosen people above all other nations on the Earth. Regardless to what a person may think about God's word, His truth will always prevail over people's opinions.

The Irony in God's Love

It's ironic that God will often show His love to us in a totally different way than we would expect or even have desired Him to. Everything the Lord does is done out of His love for us. Our minds are not equipped to understand the irony in God's love because we are only human. Just as the Heavens are higher than the Earth, so are His ways higher than our ways, and His thoughts higher than our thoughts. It's ironic that the Lord would let a pit bull maul my only child to death, but ultimately, my child went to Heaven. See what I mean? What seems contradictory to love is actually how God shows us His love.

Ironic situations happen to us all throughout our lives. If you love the Lord, the Bible says that all things are working together for the best possible outcome for your life. In other words, if you could go back to a certain situation and reverse it to what you had expected or intended, it would not have worked out in your favor in the fullness of time. Another example of an ironic situation happened to my family in the year 1968. Out of love, the Lord had a strategic plan of moving us to a new home in a better neighborhood.

I remember the Sunday afternoon when my parents gave us the option of going to church with them or staying home. My siblings and I chose to stay home that day and play. However, we went against the house rules and had company over while our parents were away serving the Lord. A fire broke out and burned our house down to the ground that faithful Sunday evening. We all got a real spanking the next day, but in the long run, it all turned out for the best for our entire family.

We lived with our grandmother for a few months, but our family eventually moved to a new house in a better neighborhood. The irony of the situation in which we found ourselves in, turned out for the best. God's love paved the way for our happy family to move into a new air-conditioned home with indoor plumbing. My parents being caught up in the moment of receiving that dreadful phone call at Church, and rushing home to see if all of their children were okay was devastating to say the least, but in the final analysis, we appreciated the irony in God's love.

God shows His love for us in baffling ways we could never understand. It's not an accident that all the people we meet are crossing our path for God's purposes. For the Lord's intentions, He places people in our daily lives for our own development, as well as for the development of the person that's interacting with us. God's actions always have a multipurpose. He doesn't seem to do anything for just one reason.

In an ironic twist, the Lord always acts out of love expecting us to follow His lead by treating problematic personalities the way we want to be treated, as opposed to the ways we are mistreated by them. There are many lessons that God wants us to learn from different people. There is nothing to be learned from treating people as cruelly as they treat you. On the other hand, there is an irony and a lot to be learned from treating offensive personalities with dignity and respect.

In this world, the rich treat the poor with less dignity and respect than they deserve. Yet, all must answer to the Lord for how we treat His people. There is an irony existing between the very wealthy and the very poor. It really doesn't matter how many changes are made in social disparities, there will always be a great wealth divide in this world. Speaking of inequality, there are three classes of people in today's society. The three classes are known as the lower, middle, and upper. The larger percentage of people (the middle) are the working class. Sometimes two jobs are required just to make ends meet.

Often being poor forces people to live together and work together in order to survive. These lower-class people are the individuals suffering financially to stay afloat. They have to choose this over that and so forth, in order to supply family necessities. The lower class have to ration out the monies they have to be financially prepared for future emergencies. They are considered the poor. Moving on up a notch, the white-collar workers fall in the middle. They are a lot more relaxed financially. They have the options of patronizing other businesses and purchasing other things outside their necessities, without suffering the future backlash for unnecessary spending.

The smallest percentage, rich people, are in the upper class. This elite group of people have enough disposable income to buy as much of anything they desire, or do anything they want to do without the worry of having insufficient funds. It's a paradox indeed that the Oxfam Report shows that the richest 1 percent of the world's population (the upper class) is worth more than the lower and middle classes' 99 percent combined. One of the downsides of being very wealthy is that false feeling of not needing anyone in your life. Many take it a step further feeling as though they don't need God because they already have money.

The rich say, "What can God do for me that money can't?" They elevate themselves above everyone and everything, including the laws of the land. The judicial system often let them buy their way out of trouble. People tend to idolize individuals that are in the upper one percent. To break a prideful spirit, the Lord may let a person live well into old age just to show an individual that they need His help, as well as, the help of other people in their life. The irony comes back around to the wealthy when they grow old in years and have to depend on others to do the simple things in life. Things that a person can no longer do due to aging.

It is sufficient here to reiterate that out of love the Lord chastens His Chosen Ones more severely than any other nation of people on Earth. Ironically, the Israelite nation of people whom God created above all other nations, He allows to be stepped on and treated like the dirt He used to create us from. While the Israelites are being persecuted by the other nations, the Lord laughs at their calamity. He laughs because He knows that all the Israelites have to do is simply obey His word. *"But ye have set at naught all my counsel, and would none of my reproof: I also will laugh at your calamity: I will mock when your fear cometh"* (Proverbs 1:25–26).

It's like when someone throws a rubber snake down in front of you. It's funny to the person that throws the snake attempting to scare you. In correlation, it is the Lord who sends our enemies to us. Since we were created to have dominion over all things on Earth, when we become afraid of anything, it makes the Lord laugh. "He did not give us a spirit of fear; but of power and of love, and of a sound mind."

Our calamities that He laughs at may seem to last a long time to us. Even lasting for years. Yet, since one day of the Lord's time is a thousand years in our lifetime, He only chuckles at our calamities for a few moments in His day. As parents, we spent a lot more time than that laughing at our own children's calamities for being disobedient. We sometimes tell our children, "I told you so," while laughing at them.

Another example of the irony in God's love is also seen in how God hates Esau, yet out of love, He sent His only begotten Son, Jesus Christ, to die so that all nations of people could have a right to eternal life. Many people would have desired that the Lord would let Esau and His nation of people, the Edomites, all perish in the eternal fire for the things they are doing and for the things they have done to the Israelites. However, since everything that the Lord does is done out of love, He created a pathway that anyone could follow that would lead them to Him, regardless of their nationality. Nevertheless, the Edomites are not quite out of the woods yet. They must repent for the mistreatment as well as the atrocities being placed upon the Israelites.

God shows His emotions to us, just as He laughs at our calamities, He also cries when the right situation presents itself. I'm sure that the Father wept for His Son before He was born to the Virgin Mary in Bethlehem. What father would not weep for his only begotten son knowing that He was about to be spat upon, beaten, whipped, mocked, and tried without justice? The Bible even says that Jesus wept, but He volunteered to die for all nations anyway. *"Jesus wept"* (John 11:35). From the very beginning, the Father knew that by sending His Son to establish that pathway it would put Jesus in the position to be mistreated, just like He knows the Israelites are still being mistreated today in Arsareth/America.

The irony here, of course, is that even though the Lord said in Malachi 1:3 that He hates Esau, on the other hand, God loved Esau so much that He would send His only begotten Son, Jesus Christ, to die for Esau and his future generations. He left the Holy Spirit here to comfort everyone in every nation. It's ironic that with all the things going on in the world, God expects us to focus on the good. The same nation of people who oppressed the Israelites are now marching side by side with them and fighting for the equality of people of color. Not even God wants us to turn a blind eye to social injustices and systemic racism.

Chapter 9

Today in History

Another pivotal moment in history has arrived. Happening on Sunday August 23, 2020, in Kenosha, Wisconsin, Arsareth/America, Jacob Blake, a twenty-nine-year-old Israelite, was critically wounded by the Edomite police officer, Rusten Sheskey. The unarmed Black man Jacob Blake was shot in the back seven times leaving him paralyzed from the waist down. This attempted murder happened in broad daylight with Jacob's three children inches away from him, while other spectators looked on. Again, a domestic violence report sparked another senseless shooting by a White police officer. As mentioned in chapter 5, I must reiterate that being Black in America, we must learn to resolve our own domestic disputes.

In Jacob Blake's case, during a family dispute his girlfriend called the police department and reported that Jacob was not supposed to be there. In hindsight, this family should have settled their own dispute without relying on police officers to do it for them, because Blake is now paralyzed. Still happening, time and time again, Black citizens call on Edomite police officers to settle their disputes between family members. What usually happens next? A family member ends up being shot seven times in the back by a scared and hateful Edomite police officer attempting to legally murder another Black person in the streets.

Jacob Blake survived the attempted murder. I'm using the term "legally murder" because certain groups of people actually believe that shooting a person in the back seven (7) times is justifiable. If it is justifiable, then it is legal. Flip the same table and let a Black woman police officer shoot a White woman in the back seven times and see if it will be called justifiable. I mean, to me, it just doesn't make any sense! Let's say for instance you are driving along in your car and another car plows into you from behind.

You expect justice from the law, don't you? In traffic court, the person that hit you from the back will be charged every time without question.

It's the principles of the matter. Police departments seem to have the right to repeatedly shoot a human being in the back and get away with it through the American judicial system. Yet, on the other hand, no one has the right to run into another person's car from the rear and not be charged for the crime. It's sad, but appropriate to say that the American judicial system respects inanimate objects more than they do live human beings.

Even though Israelites being gunned down by police is nothing new, what happened four days after the shooting on Wednesday, August 26, 2020, is new. The professional ball players felt they needed to do something and started dedicating their lives to making a difference on the legal issues of social injustice. National Basketball Association team, the Milwaukee Bucks, who is ranked number 1 in the Eastern Conference chose to boycott their game 5 playoff game against Orlando Magic.

At their pivotal point, the team cited Jacob Blake as the straw that broke the camel's back for their lack of further tolerance of social injustice. Another unarmed Black man was senselessly shot by a White police officer seven times in the back, in the state they represent as a professional team. The Milwaukee Bucks shocked the sports world by refusing to exit their locker room at game time. With the support of the National Basketball Association and their fellow players, history was made.

Not only was game five of the playoffs cancelled for the Bucks versus Magic, but the four other teams scheduled to play on national television Wednesday night also decided to stand in solidarity with the Milwaukee team. The Los Angeles Lakers who are ranked number one in the Western Conference; their opponent, the Portland Trailblazers; and the Houston Rockets scheduled to play at Oklahoma City Thunder all decided to boycott their games. If this wasn't historic enough, six Women National Basketball Association teams also cancelled their games and ten Major League Soccer teams also refused to play.

To the dismay of millions, Major League Baseball (America's game), postponed three games. The Milwaukee Brewers, based forty-five minutes away from where Blake was shot, decided not to take the field to play the Cincinnati Reds. The Los Angeles Dodgers and the San Francisco Giants also followed suit. Having the most number of Black baseball players (10) in MLB, the Seattle Mariners took a stand against police brutality toward Blacks by boycotting their game with the San Diego Padres.

Even in a predominately White sport, like tennis, the shockwaves were felt. Naomi Osaki, the young Black woman champion tennis player, also participated in the boycott. Naomi said, "As a Black woman, I feel as though there are much more important matters at hand that need immediate attention, rather than watching me play tennis." In this great historical moment, she sees things in their right perspective. It's because Naomi stepped up to the plate fighting for racial injustice, that the Western and Southern Open, the preliminary tennis tournament to the US Open, cancelled all play on Thursday.

For many years Israelites have complained about systemic racism and social injustice, but the events that took place on Wednesday and Thursday with billions of dollars of sports revenue at stake is one of the first steps that needed to be taken in order to get the 8-ball rolling. As a society, we have been brainwashed into believing that old, overused cliché stating, "It's going to take more time," and "Laws can't change overnight." It's been over sixty years since MLK was fighting the same fight. If we really want to see laws changed and quickly reformed, keep putting your hands in the White man's pocket and keep pulling out his money. That is the one and only way to reach the finish line. Sadly, athletes are not able to maintain their boycotts. The professional sports players are just like you and me. We want and need to get paid our monies in order to maintain our lifestyles. Society needs to be entertained, but the racist laws also need to be changed.

Sports and entertainment will always be more important to society than injustices here in Arsareth/America. Entertainment prevails! When it really comes down to making the sacrifice for change in the United States, money talks. Once the owners of professional sporting teams call the meeting and lay everything on the table—either you play the game, or we are going to get someone else that will play our game for us. Either you are in, or you are out of the game. Which will it be? The players have no other option than to play the White man's game.

First of all, we must understand that it will take a lot more than professional game players in the sports world to bring about social changes. While society, along with athletes, continue to dance around the problem, the real and only solution to the problem would be for the people in all fields of the entertainment industry to boycott entertainment, long enough to hurt the billionaires that own the entertainment industry. The billionaires would then consult their secret societies along with government officials of justice in the United States and have laws quickly changed to abolish injustices in order to keep growing the multibillion revenues of the entertainment world. Because millions of people in the various fields of entertainment can't afford to leave their jobs long enough to enforce changes in society, for the nation of Israelites to believe in changes for justice, we would be living a fairy tale as we wait many more decades for changes to take place in Arsareth/America.

Here is where the problem lies. "Blood Money!" As of today, there are 614 known billionaires collecting money and living on the land that was stolen from the Israelites. The stolen land is known as Arsareth/America. It's no secret and we all know the history and the method used for seizing the land that belonged to the Israelites. With the seizing of the Israelite's land came prosperity and that blood money is now firmly planted in the hands of the Edomites.

The point of issue is recognizing disparities. Disparities among nations arises when the richest 1 percent of the population in the world owns half of the world's wealth. There are around 8 billion people on the globe. Oxfam reports that there are sixty very wealthy people in the world that possess the same wealth as half of the globe. That's the state of the world in which we live in today. What sense can you make out of the fact that sixty people have the same wealth as 4 billion people? On top of that, there is an increasing gap between the very rich and the remainder of the world's population.

The wealthy people influencing the important decisions and running this country don't always have what we would consider to be a sound mind. It's contagious because sometimes the majority of people in governmental offices have that same mentality. The leaders are the ones having a great influence over how society is being run, regardless of their state of mind. With that being said, the only way to fix the problem of racial injustices and disparities, without many more decades of useless protesting and boycotting, would be to elect the right president with the proper backing of the Senate and Congress for Arsareth/America.

We would first need a president that would dedicate his or her term in office to tearing down the structures and laws that support racial disparities and injustices of the people of color. In conjunction to having the right president, there would have to be a change in the heart of the society as a whole. We would have to work together as one. That's not likely to happen! Welcome to the "rabbit hole." A new law for eradicating injustice and change is sent to Congress and the Senate, but the Edomites vetoes the new law, again. Are you surprised? Maybe now is the time to try a new approach, because Congress and the Senate are not working for people of color. History has confirmed these facts for centuries now. With all that's going on in the world today, the Lord is speaking and trying to tell us something. The Lord may very well be at His pivotal point demanding the full attention of all nations right now.

Readdressing Entertainment

Allow me to take you behind the scenes of sports and entertainment. In a perfect world, the true purpose of sports and entertainment is for the mind and bodily exercise to help maintain good health. *"For bodily exercise profiteth little: but godliness is profitable unto all things, having promise of life that now is, and of that which is to come"* (1 Timothy 4:8). However, because of Satan and sin, we were exiled from the Garden of Eden and no longer live in the perfect world that God created for us. After Adam and Eve followed Satan's lead into sin, their future generations let the prince of this world influence their ways of thinking, and through his hidden agenda, Satan puts a new spin on reality as we live out our daily lives. Let's take a broader look at what sports and entertainment means today.

Out of the love of money, the owners and organizers of the games entice and recruit the best players in the world with very large sums of money in order to draw very large crowds of people into the leisure activity of praising the games. It's not the player's fault that they are being praised above God by millions of people around the world. Neither is it the fault of the owners and organizers of sporting games and entertainment. It's Satan and his hidden agenda causing the deception of the purpose of sports and amusement. Out of the love of money, the primary goal of world sports and world entertainment organizations are to become multibillionaires. On the flip side of the coin, the goal of Satan is to distract billions of people from serving the Lord. It happens every single day of our lives, people spend a lot more time and money on worldly entertainment than being focused on the Lord.

When it comes to prioritizing what's most important to God and to society, our deeply rooted need for pagan entertainment plays a major role in the cause of the many problems we face in the world today. The Stockholm syndrome of falling into the trap of pagan entertainment has been passed down to every generation and nation of people across the globe as the great distraction from God. When nations of people become distracted from God the Lord being in full control will bring the people to their knees. The fact is, life itself is intended by God to be a spiritual journey of togetherness. As humans, our focus should be on serving the Lord in preparation for eternal life. Our life down here on Earth is not intended to be a competition to see who can gain more material things than others.

By competing against each other, it only creates division among ourselves. Yet, like all other animals in the wild, we are naturally competitive creatures. Beginning from thousands of years back, large crowds of people gathered in places for the purpose of witnessing competition between other people. I can remember as a child growing up in the '60s and '70s, we would draw crowds from far and wide by announcing the fight that would take place between two people after school. It was always exciting to see someone get beat up in the streets. It was amusing.

Stemming from biblical days as far back as 776 BC, the pagan Olympic Games were first featured in the ancient Coliseum. Large crowds of Edomites would gather for the Roman Olympic Games that featured Christians and Israelites being ripped apart by a variety of wild animals. The violent genocide of Christians and Israelites drew larger and larger crowds as the recreation got worse and worse. Thespians, singers, and musicians were featured in the ancient amphitheaters. From biblical times, the pagan entertainment and sports competition over the years became a lucrative part of world culture.

As a society, we have become brainwashed into using all forms of pagan amusement as a means of escaping from our spiritual obligations as people in conjunction with turning away from the morality of the Lord. One of our modern-day false gods, which is an idol to many, is known as technology. Spending many hours a day watching television, playing video games, or on a cell phone talking to and contacting people on social media, yet spending only a couple of minutes thinking about or talking to your God should raise a red flag in your mind. Our attention is being diverted from the Lord through many forms of worldly amusement.

The Lord's primary concern is the salvation of the nations. Pagan festivities have desensitized the nations from the things that are approved of by God. All the distractions, the screaming, clapping of hands, glorifying people on television as opposed to Him has become acceptable. Murder, theft, rape, fornication, and so forth are the types of things people are focused on today. Nations are dedicating 99 percent of their free time focused on worldly entertainment, and less than 1 percent of their time communicating with the Lord.

The Lord does not play games in Heaven for amusement, neither did Jesus play games here on Earth for fun. Jesus said: "Thy will be done on Earth as it is in Heaven." In other words, the Lord is the only one, worthy of being praised in Heaven, and on the Earth. When it comes to material things, nothing is worthy of being praised. However, money is valued and praised over the Lord. By vehicles of pagan entertainment, people, and things are being praised; and God is being placed on the back burner. It's time for all nations to move away from what God despises and be willing to exchange it for that which is relevant to the Lord.

The Lord knows that pagan vehicles of amusement, such as television, sports, clubbing, drinking, secular music, theatre, etc. are deadly distractions from the spiritual reality of our lives, and He will do anything to fix the problem. Through the cunningness of Satan, pagan recreation has gone from the violent genocide of Christians and

Israelites being ripped apart by wild animals to the spiritual genocide of Christians and Israelites being distracted from the things of God through the pagan vehicles of leisure activity. The only way that nations can solve all the problems in the world is for us to love the Lord with all our heart, soul, and mind. After all, that is His greatest commandment.

The Unity of Nations

One nation under God was Plan A before disobedience to God caused humankind to be exiled from the Garden of Eden. The Lord's Utopia or Plan A has now become Plan B, which is being born into and living in a world full of sin and chaos. The coming together of all 195 countries of people living in this world today is not God's plan. Instead, He said there would be wars and rumors of wars. One nation under God would be an ideal world to live in however, because of our disobedience, the Lord never mentioned us living this Utopian dream in His prophesy until New Jerusalem.

I've heard the same question being asked time and time again. The question is, "Why can't we all just get along?" Allow me to address this question by simply asking another. How could we expect to learn how to get along with society as a whole when we had never learned how to get along with the Lord? It's first things first. In order for all the nations of the world to unify as one, they would have to love the Lord with all their heart, soul, and mind, and love thy neighbor as thyself. What are the chances of that happening?

All the nations on the Earth, one hundred and ninety-five (195) countries came out of the seed of Abraham. Abram whom God changed his name to Abraham, was the Hebrew Patriarch of the Black Israelite nation of Jews first, then the Gentiles. Jews were the first to be created and later came the Gentiles. The Lord spoke to the Israelite Jew named Abraham and said, *"And I will make thy seed to multiply as the stars of heaven, and will give unto thy seed all the countries; and in thy seed all the nations of the Earth be blessed"* (Genesis 26:4). The problem is that the Edomites want to be above all other nations on the Earth, but God through His law has already established that position with the Israelites.

In order for the nations to unite as one, the first and most important step would be for the world to recognize that the Lord has placed the nation of Israelites on His pedestal. By the Lord creating the Israelites above all the other nations on the Earth, it's made the other nations feel uncomfortable about the Israelites' status. Some of the nations are in total disagreement with God's laws concerning the Israelites. The Edomites disagreeing with the Lord's laws decided to place themselves high upon a pedestal through their systemic laws of White supremacy against the nation of Israelites as well as others. That is the state of the world we live in today.

However, the uniting of all nations before the return of Christ is possible, only in the land of make believe. The Lord made it clear and said, that there will be wars and rumors of wars before the second coming of the Lord. So don't get caught up believing the fairy tale that other nations are going to do the right thing when it comes to eradicating social injustice and systemic racism. The battle is not ours. It's the Lord's. We, as people, have to face reality and realize that the fight for justice and equality among nations will continue until the last man is standing and only God can and will bring justice and equality to His Chosen Nation, the Israelites.

Knowing what the Bible says about the Edomites yet still being optimistic that the same people that has oppressed the Israelites for hundreds of years are suddenly going to change is irrational. Can a leopard change its spots? It has never happened before! We should not make the mistake of concluding that police officers have decided to stop racial profiling during traffic stops. Racial profiling is a part of the legal judicial system in the United States. It's difficult for the Edomites to learn how to think rationally about other races, when the temperament of hate against the Israelites has been engraved into their minds.

Reflecting on my personal experience: During a traffic stop in Greensboro, North Carolina, two police vehicles carrying four White police officers pulled me over for no apparent reason. Two officers came to the driver's door and the other two went to my passenger door. The first officer asked me to show him my registration. In response, as I slowly opened my glove compartment (filled with nothing but papers), the officer standing by the passenger side drew his gun and pointed it in my direction. If I had not been calm or made any sudden moves, that senseless traffic stop could have turned deadly. By using my common sense, I lived to see another day with my family and friends.

Take my word for it, when I tell you that being a Black male in America means when a police officer pulls you over, do exactly as instructed and don't make any sudden movements in or out of your vehicle. To be on the safe side, never carry anything shiny or reflective in your glove compartment. It could be mistaken as a weapon and an officer could open fire. Always listen carefully to their instructions and don't be argumentative. It's difficult for a White or certain segments of police officers to think rationally when they feel afraid or superior to other people.

Let's touch on the subject of police reform. People are acutely aware that today's police officers are in dire need of being reinstructed on new ways of handling situations in a civilized manner. Yet the Trump administration still refuses to admit that there is systemic racism in law enforcement. Again, just recently it's been reported that more White police officers have either strangled or put numerous bullets into another unarmed Black citizen resulting in death.

It's time to take another ride on the rusty merry-go-round of justice in America. After another senseless murder the case is presented before the judicial court system. The final nail in the coffin was driven when the Department of Justice allowed more White police officers to get away with another murder of an innocent Black citizen. Then, allowing them to roam freely like wild animals in the wilderness in search of their next prey. Taking into consideration that human beings are a class of animals, police officers behaving like wild animals need to be tamed in the same manner that wild animals are.

These improperly trained, inhumane police officers must be domesticated. They should be kept in captivity (jail) for an extended period of time for their crimes, like any other citizen. Why aren't these officers on death row? In many cases, wild animals are put down for attacking and killing human beings. I find it appropriate to say, "What's good for the monkey is good for the gorilla." For no reason at all, Blacks are being killed in the streets by so-called professional police officers. Just like wild animals involved in an attack on human beings, euthanasia should be policy for these police predators seeking out humans as prey.

Speaking of police predators, hundreds of innocent men, mostly Black, have been hunted down, captured, and received capital punishment by way of the electric chair. Over seven hundred people have been executed by way of electric chair in the past fifteen years in the United States, mostly Black men. Being put to death in an electric chair is more inhumane than the methods used for wild animals being euthanized. Maybe the lives of police officers are valued above the citizens they are paid to protect. Is it that police officers operate above the law? It's up to the courts, legislatures, and society as a whole to make that call or continue to deal with the status quo of senseless executions committed by police officers all across America.

When I first heard that the Trump Administration announced that systemic racism does not exist in law enforcement, I was shocked and appalled. Yet we all know about the existence of racial profiling in law enforcement... The first thing that came to mind was more propaganda from the Trump Administration. The American president (Donald J. Trump) and his supporters (many of whom are White supremacist) are trying to hide and downplay systemic racism. That's why millions of people living across America acknowledging systemic racism and police brutality are taking it to the streets in protest. As a Black man having my experiences with police officers in Texas, North Carolina, and California, I strongly disagree with the Trump Administration. The Edomite, Attorney General William Barr, announced on CBS Face the Nation Sunday August 30,

2020, that systemic racism does not exist in law enforcement.

Looking through tunnel vision, the attorney general can't see that the judicial system that enforces the laws in America acquit White police officers for killing unarmed Black men and women. Many officers have immunity when involved in shootings. If that's not systemic racism, like Senator and Vice-President Nominee Kamala Harris said on CNN's State of the Union on Sunday August 30, 2020: "They spend time in a different reality." A different reality? She's being polite. They have their heads buried in the sand! President Donald Trump and Attorney General William Barr actually believe that a Black male in America would receive the same treatment as they would when being pulled over by a White police officer. In reality, they wouldn't even be treated equally to the average White man because they are both rich and powerful people.

The Changing of the Guard

The message from Generation Z is: The world is yours. You are the generation of people that will gain dominion over the Earth. As it is written, one generation is born and another generation passes away. The flaming torch of justice is being passed down from the Millennials to Generation Z. While past generations take a back seat, the new outspoken Generation Z will be the guards establishing the new law and order of justice in Arsareth/America. The new bolder generation, born after the Millennials, are far from being submissive to the unjust laws that paves the way for injustice among their upcoming generation of people. They are an outspoken justice-minded new generation of citizens. As we can see from the current Black Lives Matter Civil Rights Movement, Generation Z are a courageous society of people.

Making up around one quarter of the US population, Generation Z being hopeful and optimistic are leading the civil rights movement and refusing to have their voices silenced by older generations having unrealistic views or road blocks passed down to them. They are fighting for real and lasting change. The new generation are unconquerable and are enough young people to provoke a real difference. While the powers that be tried to pull the wool over the eyes of the Baby Boomers and Generation X, the heads of Generation Z, empowered by the support of the Millennials, are not buried in the sand.

They can see what's happening and have pragmatic views on racism and police brutality. They are protesting for police, education, wage, and health reforms. Having been born into the technology that produced the information age, Generation Z has always had access to computers and cell phones teaching them the things past generations could only wonder about. Because they now know the truth, they are unyielding and will not give in to the political bull and propaganda being shoved down their throats through the media and current administration. Being responsible for and taking on the task of having the current administration changed for the sake of justice, falls squarely on the shoulders of Generation Z.

The older gray-haired generation have no choice but to listen to the youngsters. Baby Boomers grew up fighting for justice and brought forth the children of Generation X and the Millennials. Their time, as well as their energy, used on fighting for justice is far spent. At some point during the aging process, the Baby Boomers grew tired of fighting. Fighting is for the youthful, and we all know that the young will eventually win the fight over time. The seventy-year-old plus Baby-Boomer commanders-in-chief and leaders across the globe shall lose their rights to unjustly rule nations of people once they can no longer fight off the younger and stronger Generation Z. Aging is inevitable, and if one continues living, the new generation will have to care for all the other generations, as they slowly fade into the sunset of life and time.

Being young, full of energy, absolutely fearless, and armed with perseverance, Generation Z are now in the position to eradicate injustice for the sake of a better world and quality of life for our grandchildren and their children as well. Being insurmountable, feeling invincible and thinking about their own future, this new generation won't just give in to a life of injustice and inequality because they have already seen the ill effects it's having on their parents, their friends and them. The new upcoming leaders of Generation Z that will lead the nations are being molded as we speak. Taking notes of the mistakes made by our present leaders, in hindsight, Generation Z's upcoming achievers are aware that current leaders should not fuel racism and inequality, causing division among the people.

Generation Z are not working alone in their fight for racial equality. Millennials who started the Black Lives Matters hashtag on social media in the summer of 2013, paved the way to give young people a political voice following the emotionally charged unjust murder of Trayvon Martin by a wannabe-cop, neighborhood watch person George Zimmerman. Alicia Garza, Patrisse Cullors, and Opal Tometi's online network expression has given way to a full-blown movement. Street demonstrations using the moniker, "Black Lives Matter" started in 2014, protesting the senseless shooting and choke hold deaths of unarmed Michael Brown and Eric Garner at the hands of White police officers.

The Caucasians being protected by their unjust laws were swiftly acquitted for the unjust killings of the unarmed Israelites.

Sink or swim time. It's now or never. It is the moment of truth. Millennials are relentlessly fighting for human activism, feminism, immigration reform and economic justice because they have reached their height of discomfort physically, emotionally, and spiritually and have decided to address the issues behind their pain.

The Israelites having to deal with people in leadership roles that refuse to behave themselves in an ethical manner has caused hurt. Having being put in place for centuries now, the axis of injustice rotating around systemic racism in the United States is still the primary issue behind the hurt. So the Millennials, being bold enough to address these social issues in today's diverse society, have taken the first step in the healing process of a hurting nation of people. Now it's up to the upcoming Generation Z to carry the flaming torch of justice and demand solace for their ancestors and for their future children.

Chapter 10

Social Vanity and the Pride of Life

People were actually meant to live forever, and the Bible says that many of us eventually will. However, for now, everything we can see and all that we own one day will be totally worthless to us beyond our graves. The majority of people will not make it out of here alive. We must all pass away and face our mortality one day. All the things that we have worked for we will someday leave behind for someone else to enjoy. Most people in our society are living a life of self-absorption, not realizing the importance of sharing the blessings of God. Failing to realize that we have to look outside ourselves, we fall into the deadly trap of vainness. We think that what we have, we earned, and it did not come from God.

Everything we have is a gift from God. It's not about us, it's about the Lord who gave it. Even though we all need self-worth and self-esteem, it's our over-inflated ego that causes us to live our lives being excessively prideful in ourselves and in our achievements; not acknowledging Christ making it possible. For the most part, people in general are so preoccupied with themselves that they neglect to see the importance of the accomplishments made by Christ for our immortality.

The fact is that when people in societies live their lives outside of having faith in Christ, they will experience an emptiness inside. They'll spend their lives trying to fill that void with money, drugs, alcohol, and with the things that money may bring. Many family members accomplish more than the others without sharing their family blessings. As for that family, divided we fall or together we stand tall. Everyone wants the biggest house and the newest car. Which will all be pointless, in a sense, at the sunset of one's life. As we live our lives in vanity, "I want the things you have, and you want the things that I have." Which is better? In our society, it's like the blind leading the blind when it comes to acknowledging what's really worth having. Society looks upon material things as opposed to looking within themselves to measure things of true worth. Having Christ in your heart is that which is to be valued above all.

Society has a problem with being prideful. Being self-centered we are not giving the Lord the credit. We should not go around believing or even saying, "I woke myself up this morning," "I fed myself," and so on. Instead of Me, Myself, and I, it should be the Father, the Son, and the Holy Spirit. For the Holy Trinity encompasses all the power, and we, in reality, have none. The power of God trumps over all others. Power in our society is usually seen as those who possess the most currency. To some, money defines who we are. Therefore, as we grow older, instead of learning how to love God, we learn how to love money in His place.

From childhood, we were all brought up believing we need money for getting the things we want. As children we knew that the more money we had, the more candy and toys we could buy, and nothing is worth more to a child than toys and candy. From childhood, our minds have been programmed into focusing on money and material things for six days a week. Then, we focus on needing God only on Sundays. As adults, our mindset usually remained the same even though our values have changed. We had gone from candy in preschool, to cars in high school. Later in life, as full-grown adults, the amount of money we have access to would determine the type of neighborhood we could live in.

Loving money and things in oppose to loving God is actually a meaningless vanity. However, it is a powerful tool used to buy all the perishable material things needed in life. On the other hand, the power of God created all things and gives us something that can't be purchased with any amount of money, everlasting immortality. *"He that loveth silver shall not be satisfied with silver; nor he that loveth abundance with increase: this is also vanity"* (Ecclesiastes 5:10). What we failed to realize and understand as children, and sometimes as adults, is that every good and perfect gift comes from God. These gifts from God are given to us in order to bless us and teach us to share with others.

Sharing helps to teach us to have compassion for others. Being self-centered, not loving God, and having an inflated ego makes it difficult to share with others. The truth is that everything that we think we worked so hard to obtain, that we think belong to us, are actually gifts from God that still belong to Him. The only thing that any human being actually owns are the words they have spoken, and the ways that they have treated people all the days of their lives. No one actually owns more than anyone else. We all come in Earth's front door with nothing, and leave out Earth's back door with the same thing, nothing.

That's why God hates pride. He knows that everything belongs to Him. The Lord sees people in society walking around with their heads in the air, thinking they are better than others around them. Considering their gifts, they feel they are more important than other people. Their overinflated egos make it impossible for them to humble themselves to the one who owns everything and everyone on Earth. Refusing to be humble in their spirit and in their manner, their pride distracts them from having compassion and empathy for others. We should protect our offspring from falling into that distorted state of mind. Children as well as adults should constantly be reminded that "the Earth is the Lord's and the fullness thereof."

Being humble is the opposite of being prideful. A humble nation of people will accomplish things of the Lord while the prideful nation will fail. A society that has learned to show a modest estimate of their importance are seen as being humble. Social bonding throughout our nations of people will become a breeze when the people have learned how to show humility toward each other. Most people enjoy being around young children because they are naturally humble. Correspondingly, the Lord enjoys us when we learn to humble ourselves before Him, and before humankind.

The Lord is set on righting the wrongs between the nations. He will exalt the nations whom humbled themselves and served the other nations. At the same time, the Lord is going to humble the nations that has exalted themselves above the other nations. In the end, the humble nations that were forced to serve others shall rise up, and the prideful nations that led other nations into captivity shall be taken into captivity.

Reaping What You Sow

You reap what you sow. Future consequences of the Edomite nation of people whom descended from Jacob's twin brother, Esau, are destined to be judged for their mistreatment of God's chosen nation of people, the Israelites. The question is, "Are the Edomites still reaping the benefits of the stolen land and slave labor of the Israelite nation of whom descended from Jacob?" Rephrasing the question would be nothing but a distraction because you can look around and see that the Israelites are not in control of their native land Arsareth/America, which was the inherited land of Jacob's children. Ten tribes of Israel (Jacob's children) had already occupied the land we call America, before it was taken and renamed by the Edomites.

The sowing part was their mistreatment of Jacob's children the tribes of Israel.

Being led into captivity, the Israelites rights were relinquished when through violent attack, they lost their native land Arsareth to the Edomites. Upon surrendering, they had no active role in establishing the laws of their own land. After most of the Israelite men were killed during the taking of the land and the rest being held in captivity, mostly women and children survived. They had no say-so about anything. The Israelites individual rights and liberties being in the hands of their enemies the Edomites, gave the Israelites no protection from the White man, and their racist governmental laws established by them.

The reaping begins in the Lord's prophecy given to Obadiah in the Bible, announcing the final destruction of the Edomites as a result of their opposition to God's chosen nation of people, the Israelites. *"Behold I have made thee small among the heathen; thou art greatly despised"* (Obadiah 1:2). The relationship between the American and the Chinese presidents are frayed due to the coronavirus. China's population today is 1.393 billion while America is only 326.7 million. America's population is small compared to China and some other nations. Yet we lose over one thousand people a day to the Corona pandemic. On top of that, according to scripture, all other nations in the world will greatly despise America and its leaders.

In correlation to the prophecy of Obadiah 1:1, World War III may be looming just over the horizon when the nations rise up against America in battle. War signal indicators are now flashing red everywhere. Future consequences for America are inevitably shaped by what's taking place in the USA today. The Edomites in the United States are constantly sowing injustices upon the nation of Israelites. Therefore, they shall eventually reap the retribution for injustices from the nations sent against them.

As the wealth gap widens, civil unrest due to systemic racism and racial disparities are spreading across the globe. America and its leaders being filled with pride seems to be divided more than ever. When a nation is divided from within, it can be conquered from abroad. The United States government often seems to be dysfunctional. In reaping and sowing, you get what you deserve. There was a time when America was the most powerful nation in the world. Things have changed. Since the year 2000, America no longer has the highest Gross Domestic Product spending statistics. China has now outpaced America, putting the US behind them in second place. In the year 2020, economic slowdowns due to the pandemic have ultimately led to another recession here in the United States.

The pride in the hearts of today's nations of stiff-necked leaders often deceive them into believing that no other nation could bring their military down into submission. However, the Lord declares that He will bring down the nation that has exalted themselves as an eagle. The eagle spoken of in God's prophecy is the Edomites emblem of pride representing the United States of America. In the same scripture, Obadiah 1:4, the Lord said that he will bring down the International Space Station. The Lord knocking the ISS down to the ground with an asteroid would be classified as an Act of God. Something as simple as an asteroid could easily collide into the 459-

ton, football-field-sized space station and demolish it on impact.

We must all be aware and be fully prepared for the Second Coming of Christ. The pride of America's national wealth has made us feel invincible. Yet having financial power is no match for prophecy. Because America is utterly despised among the other nations, the time is drawing near when the leaders of other countries around the world will get together and deceive the leaders of this country in order to violently prevail against America. Going undetected, in plain sight, events will begin to unfold that will ultimately lead to the destruction of this wealthy country called America, a country which was founded on the blood of the Israelites, God's chosen nation of people.

The violence that Esau had done against his brother Jacob is the same violence the Edomites are doing to Jacob's descendants, the Israelites. As for the fugitives, there is no escaping God's justice for rejoicing over racial disparities and systemic racial injustices being placed upon the Israelites. In hindsight, the Edomites should have never came to Arsareth in the year 1492 to murder the Israelite families and lay hands on their inheritance by seizing over a billion acres of their homeland and later naming it America.

By the White man seizing the homeland of the Israelites, they seized the future wealth of the Israelites also. The Edomite fugitives should have never passed laws to legally remove the Israelites from their own land. Subsequently, we all know that much of the Edomites prosperity being enjoyed today was built on the backs of Israelite slaves from hundreds of years ago. The White man fugitives should have never mistreated God's Chosen whom He had sent to serve them as slaves. The mistreatment of slaves was done out of malice, hatred, greed, and ignorance.

The Edomites should have never hired slave-catchers to recapture the Israelite slaves that had been mistreated to the point that they ran away from their evil owners, seeking to gain their own freedom. This was the birth of the police enforcement in America and the creation of the police shield which remains the same to this day. The Lord's justice is drawing near when Israelites will truly be freed from the Edomites. The descendants of the Twelve Tribes of Jacob (the Israelites) will be redeemed back to the Creator. God's Chosen nation of people will forever repossess their land and all of their inheritance that comes with it. *"The day of the Lord is near for all nations. As you have done, it will be done to you; your deeds will return upon your own head"* (Obadiah 1:15).

I would like to take this opportunity to reiterate: "You reap what you sow." What the Edomites (the White man) have sown upon the nation of Israelites (the people of color), the Lord said in His word, they shall reap. In the end, the Israelites will prevail over the Edomites. The time is drawing near, and when it's all said and done, will the mistreatment of God's Chosen nation of people have been worth it? To the descendants of Esau, the answer will be "absolutely not." The power of God will rest upon the Israelites as they devour the descendants of Esau as the Lord has spoken in Obadiah 1:18.

God's Economy Trumps Man's Economy

Obedience will always trump over disobedience. The keeping of God's commandments is the positive force that drives the Lord's economy to flourish. God's economy of soul salvation is everlasting, while man's economy of the financial trading of its commodities is temporal. Being totally different from the commodities of trade used in man's economy, the Lord's spiritual commodities used in His economy are human souls. In God's economy, sin is the debt. The currency used in God's economy is repentance, praise, and worship, which eliminates the debts we owe.

In man's economy, the primary goal is to keep people in debt, and eventually take away what they own. On the other hand, in God's economy, His goal is to free our spirit from the debt of sin and equally share everything that He owns with everyone forever. Being obedient to the Lord's command by accepting the atonement saving grace of His Son should be humanity's ultimate pursuit here on Earth. What a contrast between the two. As from ancient times to the present, the only commodity used in God's economy are the souls of His people.

In the beginning, after God's commandments were first given to Adam and Eve, then the instructions for growing God's economy here on Earth were later given to the Israelite's Patriarch Abraham. It was Abraham that passed the Lord's Covenant down to Isaac. Then it was Isaac that passed the Covenant Laws down to his son Jacob (Israel). From Jacob's twelve (12) sons, The Twelve Tribes of Israel were formed to continue growing God's economy of saving souls.

Consequently, the disobedience of the Twelve Tribes of Israel overshadowed God's cause. A changing of the guard had to take place for the sake of saving souls. After the Israelites failed to obey God's Covenant, the Lord had to send His Son, Jesus Christ, to do what it would take to continue growing God's economy of saving souls. So the Israelite from the Tribe of Judah, Jesus Christ, having compassion for the souls of all nations of people in the world, and being obedient to the Father was the answer. Christ having compassion for the souls of humanity fulfilled the laws of His Father and lived, died, and rose for the souls of everyone, past, present, and future.

Finally, the last sin is committed and the end of time as we know it has arrived. The Accuser (Satan) has used his last opportunity to establish his lies about Christians in order to deceive the world. God's Chosen people have all accepted the Atonement of Jesus Christ as the only means of salvation. The Israelites have lived their lives as the light of the world by bringing others to Christ, and our works are now finished in the name of the Lord. The end of the world has come, and our loved ones awaits us. Our long-awaited family reunion of all our family members, along with our past acquaintances, has now become our eternal reality.

We anticipate the atmosphere in the residence of God and His angels to be a state of bliss, delight, and perfect peace. As we return to our natural spiritual habitat, Heaven, one nation under God will be indivisible. We will all share the same culture, language, and ethnic origin under one just and fair government of God. Being that the jurisdiction authority of the universe belongs to Christ, the fair and just ruling of joint inheritance will be in effect, forever. Anticipating a new life, living in our glorified bodies of eternal light, we will all merit equal distribution of the Creator's wealth. Living life in the timeless existence of eternity, and having access to the accumulated and stored treasures of God, living in true wealth will be everyone's reality.

All that belongs to Christ will belong to you and me, and all of our desires will be fulfilled in Heaven. It is an honor for a child of God to be placed at the bottom of the social hierarchy in Heaven. Living in the state of tranquility, every single entity will be at peace in the heavenly society, knowing and addressing each person by their God-given name. We will all finally live peacefully together in the Eternal Light of God, always.

However, before that time comes, there is an exceptional need for sincere repentance amongst the nations. There is not a just person upon the Earth that is without sin. Everyone will be judged. No one can escape Christ's final justice. Only the names of those not blotted out and remain in The Book of Life will be saved. Christ will blot out the names of those who failed to believe in the atonement that brings salvation to all through His grace; not by our own works of righteousness. Believing in the grace-saving atonement of Jesus Christ is the requirement for the salvation of all nations.

The mighty angels of God will prepare to come down from Heaven for the final elimination of sin from the Earth. The seven angels standing before God will be given seven trumpets to sound. One after the other, angels will begin sounding the trumpets of God causing the plagues and the judgments of God to occur. After the mighty angel proclaimed in a loud voice, "Who is able to break the seals and open the scroll?" Jesus, the Israelite from the Tribe of Judah is the only one worthy to take the scroll and open the seven seals of God's judgments.

During the course of events, the sealing of the one hundred and forty-four thousand (144,000) Israelites from the Twelve Tribes of Israel begin with four of God's angels coming down from Heaven, preventing the wind from blowing on the land and on the seas on Earth. That's when the unrepentant nations on the Earth are all killed, and God's Chosen 144,000 Israelites from the Twelve Tribes of Israel are rescued by the Lord.

The hostility on Satan's behalf, aimed at not keeping the ways of the Tree of Life, has vanished into eternal defeat. The vicious military conflict between God and Satan is over because Satan has been defeated and captured by the Lord. The Liar and his terrorist organization of evil has now been defeated and will burn forever in the eternal lake of fire and brimstone and never be consumed by the fire in Hell. The present Earth and everything in it is finally burned up in the great fire, and Man's economy is finished. The illusion of our past personal interest and goals created by our self-willed ego, and living in the enjoyment and safety of our human bodies no longer exist.

At last, everyone and everything praises and worships the Father, the Son and the Holy Spirit sitting on the royal throne. As we live in our new glorified bodies of Eternal Light, our inner peace has brought us back to the constant praising of the Creator, rather than the created. All tears have been wiped away from our eyes and there is no more death or sorrow. The climax of prophecy has unfolded. The new phenomenon has arrived. The present Earth, along with its laws of nature are burned up, and the New Earth appears along with the new and different laws. All of the oceans and seas have now become land. Prophecy prevails as the present chaotic universe has passed away.

The city of New Jerusalem comes down from Heaven to Earth. *"And I saw a new Heaven and a new Earth: for the first Heaven and the first Earth were passed away; and there was no more sea. And I John saw the holy city, New Jerusalem, coming down from God out of Heaven, prepared as a bride adorned for her husband"* (Revelation 21:1–2). Unlike in the present-day city of Jerusalem, in New Jerusalem there will be no need of the sun or moonlight to shine on it. The glory of the Father, the Son and the Holy Spirit will lighten it, forever. The light of the Lord shines brightly everywhere. The darkness of night time has become a thing of the past and will no longer exist.

Revelation 21:12–14 describes the eternal monument commemorating the Nation of Israelites. The city of New Jerusalem features a new wall, having twelve gates, and at the gates are twelve angels. To commemorate His chosen people, the Israelites, the Lord has written upon the great wall the names of the Twelve Tribes of the Children of Israel. The names of the Israelites written are, Judah, Ruben, Gad, Asher, Naphtali, Manasseh, Simeon, Levi, Issachar, Zebulon, Joseph, and Benjamin. Also written on the great wall of the city of New Jerusalem to commemorate the Israelites, are the names of the Disciples—Simon, Andrew, James, John, Philip, Bartholomew, Thomas, Matthew, James, Simon, Jude, and Judas Iscariot. These are the names of the twelve original Apostles that Jesus Christ had chosen to follow Him throughout His ministry on Earth.

As an Israelite, I am profoundly inspired and feel honored that the Creator has built an eternal monument to represent, glorify, and honor the commemoration of the nation of Israelites all throughout eternity. Built to last forever and surpassing all other monuments in beauty, the Lord uses precious stones like jasper, sapphire, chalcedony, emerald, sardonyx, sardius, chrysolite, beryl, topaz, chrysoprase, jacinth, and amethyst in its construction. However, the healing of all the nations including the Edomites, Moabites, Ammonites, and so on, are still a concern of the Lord. For this reason, the Most High God has planted the Tree of Life bearing twelve different fruits for the healing of all of the nations in the midst of the heavenly streets of gold.

The Final Call for Urgency

Being unaware of our true purpose in life, many of us have no sense of urgency while preparing ourselves for the second coming of Christ. The Lord is not at all pleased because the nations have become complacent and seem to be unaware of the signs of the end times. The Lord is not getting a sense of seriousness from us when it comes to doing what it takes to make it into Heaven. Why haven't we as nations put our shoes on yet? As a child, I can remember my parents telling my siblings and me, "Be ready to walk out the door in five minutes." Once everyone was informed, and the time had expired, anyone of us not having our shoes on and laces tied was in trouble.

It would upset our parents because we showed them no sense of urgency for the time at hand. Understanding the urgency of the situation at hand, the same principle applies with our Father in Heaven. It's imperative for all nations to act promptly, decisively, and without delay moving from complacency into action. Our sense of urgency requires acknowledging the scriptures and taking action, sooner rather than later. *Jesus said: "Repent!"* Consequences of complacency could be devastating to one's Eternal fate. *"Let us hear the conclusion of the whole matter: fear God and keep His commandments; for this is the whole duty of man. For God shall bring every work into judgment, with every secret thing, whether it be good or whether it be evil"* (Ecclesiastes 12:13–14).

The End

Being Black In America

References

The Holy Bible (King James Version)
The Apocrypha (King James Version)
The Book of Jasher
Legislative Affiliate of Family Research Council
NAACP.org
Atlanta Black Star
The Miami New Times
The Oxfam Report
CBS *Face the Nation*
CNN *State of the Union*
Wikipedia
US Census Bureau

About the Author

Myron was born in the summer of 1956, the second of seven children born to Otho and Doris Viser. He resided in Houston, Texas, until the age of twenty-two. He moved to Southern California, got married, and later moved to North Carolina. He started bodybuilding at the age of eleven, and it's still an intricate part of his life today. His first book titled *Adding for Jesus* demonstrated his love for mathematics, as well as his love for the Lord. It was published in 2007 and sold out.

Being a Black male living in America is a dichotomy to him. It is both a hardship as well as an honor. With all that's happening in today's society, he had to break his silence. He wrote this book to unearth the true history of how this country became the America that it is today. His real-life experiences and knowledge are undisputed. Myron's beliefs and convictions are deeply rooted in the King James Version of the Bible and color his perspectives. Writing this book was cathartic for him and is vividly informative to the reader.

CPSIA information can be obtained
at www.ICGtesting.com
Printed in the USA
BVHW060102110821
614096BV00018B/996